Living Yogācāra

Publisher's Acknowledgment

The publisher gratefully acknowledges the generous help of the Hershey Family Foundation in sponsoring the publication of this book.

LIVING YOGĀCĀRA

AN INTRODUCTION TO
CONSCIOUSNESS-ONLY BUDDHISM

TAGAWA SHUN'EI

TRANSLATION AND INTRODUCTION
BY CHARLES MULLER

WISDOM PUBLICATIONS • BOSTON

Wisdom Publications
199 Elm Street
Somerville MA 02144 USA
www.wisdompubs.org

Original Japanese edition published by Shunjusha Publishing Company. *HAJIMETE NO YUISHIKI* by Shun'ei Tagawa. This English edition is published with Shunjusha Publishing Company, Tokyo, in care of Tuttle-Mori Agency, Inc., Tokyo

Library of Congress Cataloging-in-Publication Data
Tagawa, Shun'ei, 1947–
[Hajimete no yuishiki. English]
 Living Yogacara : an introduction to consciousness-only Buddhism / Tagawa Shun'ei ; translation and introduction by A. Charles Muller.
    p. cm.
Originally published: Hajimete no yuishiki. Tokyo : Shunjusha Pub. Co., 2001.
Includes bibliographical references.
ISBN 0-86171-589-6 (pbk. : alk. paper)
1. Yogacara (Buddhism) I. Muller, A. Charles, 1953– II. Title.
BQ7494.S5813 2009
294.3'92—dc22
                              2009010814
13 12 11 10 09
5 4 3 2 1

Cover design by Rick Snizik. Interior design by TLLC. Set in Diacritical Garamond Pro 11/14.5.

Printed in the United States of America.

Table of Contents

Translator's Introduction

WHAT IS YOGĀCĀRA?

While Yogācāra Buddhism is fairly well known to specialist researchers in Buddhist studies, it is still basically unknown to ordinary Buddhists in Asian countries, as well as Buddhist practitioners and other nonspecialist students in the West. Why is this the case? First of all, despite the enormous influence of Yogācāra during the formative periods of Mahāyāna Buddhism in India, the school died out there—along with Buddhism in general, toward the end of the first millennium. In Tibet, despite its influence, the school never really existed as a distinct tradition. In East Asia, Yogācāra *did* exist as a distinct tradition, but for practical purposes, pretty much ceased to wield any major influence after the first millennium of the Common Era.

Despite its eventual disappearance as an independent school, Yogācāra teachings on karma, meditation, cognition, and path theory had a powerful impact on the other Mahāyāna schools that developed during the time of the importation of Yogācāra to Tibet and East Asia, such that much of the technical terminology on which other Mahāyāna schools based their discourse was absorbed from the various strands of Yogācāra.

The lack of the development of a Yogācāra school in Tibet is mainly due to the fact that it was absorbed into newly created indigenous Tibetan doctrinal schools. In East Asia, on the other hand, Yogācāra did exist for some time as an independent sect, known in Chinese as *Weishi* (consciousness-only) or *Faxiang* (dharma-characteristic). But the school ended up dying out in the face of various forms of competition with (1) doctrinal schools whose teachings were deemed more resonant with the

East Asian worldview, and (2) more popularly oriented schools such as the Pure Land and Meditation (Chan/Seon/Zen) schools that offered a form of teaching and practice much more readily apprehensible to the ordinary lay believer.

Yogācāra's greatest obstacle in terms of gaining widespread popularity resided in the complexity of its unwieldy system of viewpoints, paths, and categories, explained in difficult technical terminology. It does, indeed, require a fairly significant degree of commitment on the part of the student to attain a level of basic understanding sufficient to read and comprehend a Yogācāra scripture.

There are some, however, who would argue that this perceived difficulty in understanding Yogācāra may also lie to a great extent in the manner of presentation, and I'm sure that this is a view of the matter that the author of the present book, Tagawa Shun'ei, would wholeheartedly endorse. That is to say, despite the seeming unwieldy complexity of the Yogācāra system, what the Yogācāra masters are talking about in many cases are readily recognizable everyday experiences shared by all of us. Many of the points that the Yogācāra masters focused on were things that we all take for granted, but for which, when examined in greater detail, we really have no explanation. And in most cases—I believe we can add— many of these are questions for which researchers in fields such as modern psychology, physiology, chemistry, and physics do not yet have answers.

The first example that I often like to take up with my own students is the matter of memory and learning. Even the smallest children inherently know that if they try to do something the first time and don't succeed, their chances at success at a given task will continue to improve as they keep trying. This means that they know the experience of, let's say, shooting a basketball into a hoop is retained, and built upon, as a stepping stone for the next attempt. And it must be retained not only conceptually, in the gray matter of one's brain (if, indeed, that's where such information is kept), but in the fingers, hands, arms, and legs that work together in the task of taking the shot. But precisely speaking, where are these experiences being accumulated in a way that they are accessible for subsequent retrieval?

Shooting a basketball into a net is one relatively simple event in our lives. In the course of growing from children into adults, we experience, enact, and input a staggeringly vast amount of information into that which we call "memory." We have input from our parents, siblings, relatives, and friends; then, from our teachers, classmates, books; and nowadays, TV, movies, and the Internet. The amount of information that we are taking in during a single day can be staggering, not to mention it's compounding in the accumulation of months and years.

We have, of course, been taught since we were very young that items of memory are stored somewhere in the brain. If this is true, then with the brain being made of physical matter, should it not be the case that as we keep adding information, the brain should grow in size in order to contain this? Of course, it does not. But then where is all of this conceptual information being kept—not even to mention information relevant to bodily activity?

The obvious response to this question is that this information is stored somewhere in "the mind." But if this is the case, where in the mind is this vast amount of information stored? And how do we know that we are not steadily losing information at the same time? And if we are storing it, exactly how do we retrieve it when we need it? For the majority of responses, the answer is "well, we don't exactly know."

For the formulators of the Yogācāra school, this kind of answer was not acceptable, and thus they strove through their studies, research, and contemplative techniques to provide some answers, as well as a broad range of related, and even more fundamental, questions.

It must be pointed out at this juncture that the motivation for the Yogācāra researchers was not simply the creation of an early Indian Buddhist equivalent to modern cognitive or behavioral psychology. Asaṅga, Vasubandhu, and their colleagues were religious thinkers forced—through apparent contradictions and doctrinal complexities inherent in the Buddhist explanation of the nature of the human mind, juxtaposed with the processes that lead to either enlightenment or deeper entrapment in ignorance and suffering—to try to work out some solutions that were rationally apprehensible. In the process of working out such solutions (while inheriting a long-developing tradition of philosophy of the mind provided by previous scholars) they ended up needing to do a very thorough investigation of how, exactly, it is that we know things, and how, exactly, our bodies and minds change and develop. Having to deal with these kinds of issues, they could not but encounter some of the same problems that are met by modern philosophers, psychologists, and even evolutionary biologists. And it is precisely for this reason that Yogācāra studies have come, in modern times, to attract the interests of various intellectuals whose work lies outside the realm of religious faith, who study problems in cognition, human behavior, personality development, and so forth.

In the final analysis, though, the problems dealt with by the Yogācāras are Buddhist problems, through and through, and thus to understand the motivations behind the works of these thinkers, it is probably useful to provide a brief overview of how these problems developed.

No-Self

The core problem that is addressed in Buddhist doctrine and practice is that of the mistaken attachment to an imaginary notion of a "self," "ego," or "eternal soul." For according to Buddhism, it is because of the erroneously generated notion of a clearly delimited, enduring, unitary self that all troubles arise, and it is through this that human beings entrap themselves ever deeper in fictions that engender further troubles. Śākyamuni Buddha's direct discourse on this matter came in the form of the refutation of an eternal self, or soul, called *ātman,* which early Indian thinkers of his time generally regarded as the basis for the existence of all living beings. In the Indian worldview during the sixth century BCE and afterward, this ātman was understood to be the subject of the cycle of reincarnation, a cycle that only ended in the attainment of an experience of liberation, wherein individual ātmans were dissolved into their source, *brahman,* the eternal world-soul.

While on one level, we can understand the refutation of a self to be directed historically toward early Indian suppositions about an eternal ātman, the object of the deconstruction of selfhood taught in Buddhism is not limited to this particular event in Indian intellectual history—it has basically the same relevance for any culture, in any time. That is, while many of us may not have ever been formally inculcated with specific religious or philosophical doctrine advocating the existence of an "eternal self," even the most learned scientists and philosophers among us cling to a semiconscious notion, or intuition, of unitary, enduring selfhood. And for good reason, since after all, we all possess a stream of memory that goes back to our earliest childhood, providing a cohesive narrative. We have all been conditioned to identify with our own names and various first and second person pronouns since we first learned to speak. We all feel uncomfortable when disparaged, and feel good when praised. From a Buddhist perspective, this is all because we are deeply attached to an ego that we see as possessing its own inherent identity.

This ātman is always accompanied by the notion of "mine" (technically described in Buddhism as "objects of self"), referring not simply to the things one legally *owns,* but also to all the perceivable objects within one's environment. In regard to these objects, we give rise to imbalanced (and logically unsupportable) emotions of like and dislike, which further generate a whole range of afflictive feelings such as pride, jealousy, anger, attachment, and so forth. These not only bring us pain, but further impair the clarity of our thinking. In India, a wide variety of contemplative techniques would come to be developed in various doctrinal and cultural forms of Buddhism, most of which had as their ultimate goal deconstructing, or refuting, the notion of *I.* The full annihilation of egoistic identification was said to result in liberation, called in Buddhism *mokṣa,* or *nirvāṇa,* a state of cessation of afflictive mentation. A key point here is that in order for this experience to occur, it is not sufficient to simply come to intellectually understand the fictional character of the self through a logical, discursive, approach. Intellectual understanding alone is not powerful enough to change (for Buddhists) innumerable lifetimes of habituation of the I-notion. Thus, it was understood that it was necessary to work through the repeated application of meditative techniques aimed toward the dissolution of the notion of self.

IMPERMANENCE AND DEPENDENT ARISING

One basic Buddhist method of demonstrating the untenability of the notion of self is that of taking account of the impermanence (Skt. *anitya*) of all existence. We know, being educated with twenty-first century science, that all matter is in a continual state of flux. Atoms and molecules are in continuous motion, breaking down and recombining. Śākyamuni intuited this without the benefit of instruments penetrating to the microscopic layer, based entirely on his thorough inference. Following the same rigorous mental inquiry, he also stated that it was not only matter that was impermanent: there was nothing in the material or spiritual realm which could possibly exist without continuously changing. According to him, the notion of ātman as "unchanging" was untenable.

More important than *impermanence* in the task of refuting the concept of an eternal identity, however, is the Buddhist view of dependent arising. The main reason that Śākyamuni considered such a thing as the centralized entity of a "self" to be an impossibility rose from his view of the way all things arise, subsist, and cease. Śākyamuni explained that living beings do not exist as distinct, self-subsisting entities. Rather, they only come into being as provisional combinations of a vast array of causes and conditions. This mode of existence is called, in Sanskrit, *pratītya-samutpāda,* which is translated into English as *dependent arising.* He thus denied the belief in a "higher" or "more real" substance present in living beings as eternal "self" enclosed in body/mind. Rather, he saw living beings as nothing other than a vast conglomeration of complex factors: physical matter and sensory, perceptive, emotional, and psychic forces joined in a marvelous combination.

The more traditional description of dependent arising is that which was taught by Śākyamuni at an early stage in his teaching career, which elaborates the process of the construction of perception and cognition engendering birth and death in an unending cyclical fashion. This is the twelve-limbed model of dependent arising, wherein each event occurs with the prior as precondition. The twelve-linked model was used in early Indian Buddhism primarily to deconstruct the notion of a defined, eternal self. Later, the implications of dependent arising, especially as they develop in later forms of Mahāyāna Buddhism, were explained in a broader manner, more akin to the approach of modern physics, which recognizes the lack of border between things at the subatomic level. This means there was a recognition that it was not only sentient beings that do not exist as separate, monolithic entities. All of the myriad objects surrounding us also lack any kind of delimited permanent identity, only existing by virtue of dependence on other factors and conditions. The implications of dependent arising developed to include that we should both not grasp to the notion of an "I" and also not grasp to the objects that surround us. This notion of lack of inherence in the objects around us is represented in the well-known Buddhist concept of *emptiness* (Skt. *śūnyatā*).

Right View

The juxtaposition of the mistaken way of seeing oneself and things—as inherently existent, delimited entities—with the correct way of seeing things—as impermanent and dependently arisen—indicates that the most fundamental problem of human beings is that of their mistakenly habituated mode of knowing things. Thus, in Western philosophical parlance, the Buddhist problem is primarily an epistemological one, a problem that we have with our way of knowing things. Hence the investigations, research, and contemplations undertaken by the Yogācāras were centered on uncovering, demonstrating, and correcting these sorts of errors.

The Yogācāra masters can be said to have simply been carrying out a deep and elaborate extension of the basic eightfold Buddhist path, which the Buddha is said to have taught during his first sermon as the method for extricating ourselves from affliction and delusion. The first of the eight items listed in this path is that of Right View, which means, simply stated, the seeing of things as they truly are, the obvious implication being that those who are trapped in an existence marked by suffering are *not* seeing things as they truly are. Rather, their view of themselves and their world is colored and distorted by a range of mental obstructions: prejudices, attachments, assumptions, and inaccurate perceptions and conceptions of things, which are produced from the mistaken imputation of selfhood in persons and things.

Karma

Once we have a basic understanding of the notion of selflessness, we can see that logical problems must arise for Buddhist thinkers once they attempt to integrate this with the important Buddhist notions of *karma* and *trans-migration*. Karma, according to Buddhism, is the universal law of cause and effect, which can be compared, to some extent, to Einstein's law of the conservation of energy. This is to say that there is no action anywhere in the universe that does not have a corresponding reaction. There is no cause that does not have some kind of effect. However, whereas Einstein's theory was primarily directed at clarifying the function of matter and energy at the level of measurable physics, the Buddhist understanding of flawless binding of cause and effect extends into the mental realm, where all actions, speech, and thoughts are understood to possess their own qualities, or values, which engender some kind of negative, positive, or neutral/indeterminate moral effect. The moral quality of one's activities in the present moment brings about the creation of the being (oneself) who is being continually recreated in the ensuing second, minute, year—and in the case of Buddhism—lifetime. The existence of this law of karma provides the main rationale for the aspect of Buddhist practice that deals with morality.

At first glance, one might well ask what is so special about the insight that causes and effects are inextricably bound to each other. Is it not obvious? Well, it may be obvious within the limits of the measurable sensory realm. But it is certainly not obvious within the mental/spiritual sphere. There are some story writers whose works appear in books and film who regularly portray people living out their lives treating others unfairly with no apparent retribution to be seen, while others who live out their days engaged in activities characterized by generous caring are met with continuous misfortune. What guarantee is there of recompense for the deeds, words, and thoughts that one carries out? And if karma is indeed accurately transferred, if we will indeed be held accountable for all of our rights and wrongs and in-betweens, by what kind of process can this be explained? This is one problem.

The second problem associated with karma is that of transmigration. If it is supposed to be the case that beings are reborn in circumstances dictated by the quality of their prior actions, and if there is no "I," how can the process of rebirth be posited? Exactly who, or what, is being reborn? And if there is rebirth, how is individuated karma transmitted between lifetimes?

EXPLAINING THE DOCTRINE: ABHIDHARMA

Given the flourishing state of competing philosophical schools in India during the rise and development of Buddhism, Buddhist thinkers could not but be compelled to attempt to offer logically supportable answers for the problems raised above. In response to these sorts of questions, there arose a range of philosophical sects, whose doctrinal inquiries came to be known broadly in India as Abhidharma ("about the dharma"). Abhidharma became a large and diverse scholarly project that endeavored to conceptualize a theoretical background to explain the phenomena of incessant coursing through cyclic existence, along with the escape therefrom.

SIX CONSCIOUSNESSES

One of the things for which the Abhidharma tradition is noted is their investigation into the problems of causation and rebirth within the matrix of individuated consciousness. Over time, they developed elaborate schemes for explanation of these phenomena, built upon extensive technical terminology. One of the major products of their work was the articulation of a well-defined "map" of human consciousness, which they divided into six regions, according to distinct cognitive functions. This set of six is well understandable from the perspective of modern psychology and physiology, since its first five regions are none other than our five senses, with the sixth being the mind, broadly defined. The principal activity of the mind was understood to be thinking, which is carried out primarily through concepts—linguistic constructs and mental images. The faculty of mind, as it was understood by Abhidharmists, had as its principal objects (1) the perceptions received from the five sense consciousnesses, (2) language, and (3) images—both those apprehended in the present and those retained in the memory. This model was apparently satisfactory as a theoretical basis for a certain period of time. But it also presented new logical problems that required more thoroughgoing treatment. We can say that it is in response to some of these problems that the school known as Yogācāra was born.

Yogācāra and Its Various Projects

The school known as Yogācāra began to take form in the fourth century CE as both a result of continued aims at refining the theories of the mind developed by the Abhidharmists, as well as in response to certain philosophical positions found in the discourse of the competing Madhyamaka (Middle Way) school, which had carried out the most rigorous articulations of the notion of emptiness. The word *Yogācāra* is comprised of the two components *yoga* and *ācāra*. Yoga in this case refers to meditative analysis, and *ācāra* means "practice." Thus we can understand that this school arose as a system of meditative practices aimed at the attainment of liberation. The underlying motivation of the school, then, is salvific—alleviating living beings from their suffering. In the process of this work, however, Yogācāra masters also sought to articulate as comprehensive and rational an account as possible for the psychological/spiritual processes involved in the attainment of liberation.

The principal founders of the Yogācāra school are traditionally listed as Maitreyanātha, Asanga, and Vasubandhu. While concrete biographical details on the first figure are vague, the latter two, brothers who lived in India during the late fourth and early fifth centuries, are thought by scholars to be the authors of many of the most important formative texts of the tradition. The Yogācāra school later received important influences from such figures as Dignāga (c. 480–540) and Sthiramati (seventh century) before it declined in popularity in India during the eighth century and made its move to Tibet and East Asia.

The Eight Consciousnesses

Above we introduced the scheme of six consciousnesses, taken as a model for sensory and cognitive operation by early Buddhists. While this model of the five sense consciousnesses together with the sixth thinking consciousness might suffice for explaining the function of everyday waking awareness and thought in this life, there are a number of problems that present themselves. One of the more significant problems is the fact that Buddhism accepts as a basic principle the doctrine of transmigration (reincarnation), and declares, furthermore, that transmigration operates strictly by means of the flawless principle of karma. Yet we can readily see that when the body passes away, the senses will also pass away, meaning that the mental consciousness will also lose its sources of input and place of residence. Upon dying, it cannot but be the case that all six of these consciousnesses are going to disappear. In the absence of a transcendent, enduring self or *ātman,* what would be there to continue into existence into another lifetime?

Leaving aside for the moment the question of the cyclical existence of a distinct living being, how is it that we are able to maintain continued awareness of anything at all? Obviously the continuity of our mental experience is not occurring by virtue of the total, unbroken, conscious, holding-in-awareness of all thoughts and experiences through which we have passed. That would be impossible—an incredible overload of our faculties would come about almost immediately. Yet when a thought, or a sensory or emotive experience, leaves us, we are somehow able to recall it in the future, despite the fact that we do not continue to maintain it at the fore of our conscious awareness. And not only are we able to let things disappear from our consciousness and recall them again later on; we are able to accumulate distinctive forms of knowledge, as well as physical and mental skills, and are able to continue to build on these, as when we learn how to play tennis, or learn a foreign language, or calculus. Where are these batches of information, and these abilities all being put away? And how are we able to retrieve them when the need arises?

Further, assuming that the sensory and perceptual faculties of human beings all function in pretty much the same way, we can take note of the fact that a vegetable patch is seen in a radically different way by a farmer than it is by a city-dwelling office worker. The perceptions of the farmer are being deeply colored by his prior experience. But where, in this case, is the coloration coming from? Where is it being stored?

Our definition of what comprises the mind gets more complicated when we attempt to reconcile it with basic Buddhist doctrines. It also was becoming more complicated for the Abhidharmists who were trying to offer a rational and coherent explanation of the mind and human being in the context of Buddhist dependent arising, suffering, and release from suffering.

What they began to conclude was that the mind had to have at least two very distinct regions: (1) an active, manifest region that included thinking, feeling of emotion, reception and integration of sensory contact, and (2) a subliminal, subconscious aspect that had the capacity for storage and maintenance of continuity of karma, in terms of both the day-to-day experiences of the present lifetime, and the continuity of a distinct flow of apparent individuality between lifetimes. Thus an additional consciousness came to be established, a sort of root consciousness *(mūla-vijñāna)*, or adhering consciousness *(ādāna-vijñāna)*, which served as the source of continuity on which the other consciousnesses could rest.

At this point in the inquiry, we are historically beginning to move from the end of the Abhidharma approach to the problem to the birth of theories that would be seen as belonging to the Yogācāra school. After a period of time, the Yogācāra thinkers saw the need to further distinguish the base consciousness into two aspects. One aspect, which was called the *manas* (which means "mind" in a broad sense), was seen to play the role of a sort of preconscious tendency to assume the existence of an actual self, construing the base consciousness to be an ātman. This consciousness was numbered as the seventh, after the sixth thinking consciousness. Since it was the source of attachment to the notion of a self, it was also seen to be the origin of all selfish views and tendencies, thus, it was also termed "defiled consciousness" (Skt. *kliṣṭa-vijñāna*).

The remaining region of consciousness, which came to be seen as the ultimate ground of existence, was understood to be the locus of the storage and reproduction of karma and the consciousness that continued to exist after death and form the basis for the new being in the next life. It was numbered as the eighth consciousness, and called the *ālaya-vijñāna*, or "store consciousness." The resulting scheme was that of the five sense consciousnesses, the sixth, thinking consciousness *(mano-vijñāna)*, the seventh consciousness, called *manas*, and the eighth, *ālaya-vijñāna*.

OTHER EPISTEMOLOGICAL AND SOTERIOLOGICAL ISSUES

The elaboration of the minds of sentient beings into this system of eight consciousnesses represents only one portion of the topics covered by the

Yogācāra thinkers. At a more epistemological level, their concerns lay in basic problems of how cognition is possible, and how cognition bifurcates into correct and incorrect modes of activity. Numerous Yogācāra writers engaged in hair splitting analyses of the processes of cognition. Again, the lack of a distinctively delimitable "I," along with an awareness of the dependently arisen character of all things, could not but call into question commonsense reified notions of subject and object. Thus, great effort was made at trying to precisely articulate the relationship of sentient beings with their surrounding environment.

Along the way to understanding the processes leading to liberation—or, conversely, further enmeshment in ignorance and suffering—the Yogācāra thinkers also dedicated much energy to trying to understand and explain the processes of karmic causation, and how these could be concentrated in their function within separately identifiable human beings. While the scope of their interests was broad, they went to great lengths to tie all of these problems into one cohesive system.

TRANSMISSION INTO EAST ASIA

Buddhism began to trickle into China during the first and second centuries CE, and eventually began to flow rapidly into the entire East Asian region. Giving the basic weight to Buddhism as a new tradition in East Asia were the voluminous translations of Buddhist scriptural texts from Sanskrit into Chinese. At the earliest period of the transmission of Buddhism into East Asia, Yogācāra proper had not yet been born (although its Abhidharmic predecessors were hard at work). But as Yogācāra developed, its texts were also translated into Chinese, and these naturally attracted the attention of Chinese masters of the Buddhist doctrine.

Some central Yogācāra texts were translated in the fifth and sixth centuries by Paramārtha (499–569) and his contemporaries, but many among this earlier set of texts were apparently incomplete, and thus it took a fair amount of time before the Yogācāra corpus was accurately and adequately understood in East Asia. During the Sui and Tang periods, a Chinese Buddhist scholar named Xuanzang (600–664) was deeply interested in Yogācāra, and became increasingly disturbed with both the quality and quantity of the translated Yogācāra materials that were available in China. He eventually became so consumed with the matter of their rectification that he ignored an imperial edict against foreign travel and left for a seventeen-year cultural exchange in the West, most of which was spent in India.

The story of Xuanzang's famous trip to India is well known from a variety of perspectives in East Asian cultural history. When he returned to Chang'an in 645, he brought back with him wagonloads of scriptures and treatises representing all sorts of Buddhist traditions, and the subsequent translation of these texts made a profound effect on the entire East Asian Buddhist tradition. But for Xuanzang personally, the real treasures in the corpus were the Yogācāra texts, most important of which were such works as the *Saṃdhinirmocana-sūtra,* the *Yogācārabhūmi-śāstra,* and the *Mahāyānasaṃgrāha.* Xuanzang, who spent a great deal of his time in India mastering the language and the Yogācāra system, translated these with a precision and mastery unequalled in the East Asian tradition of scriptural translation. Based on his new translations, the understanding of the Yogācāra system in East Asia was dramatically transformed.

The Indian Yogācāra texts that were translated by Xuanzang and his assistants were instrumental in directing the subsequent flow of this doctrinal system in East Asia. But in terms of the influence of a single Yogācāra text on the East Asian tradition, there was none equal to that of the *Cheng weishi lun [CWSL],* composed by Xuanzang and his disciples as an attempt to systematize the main points of the Yogācāra teachings into a single work. While certain parts of the *CWSL* drift from the doctrinal positions put forth in the *Yogācārabhūmi* and other texts, the *CWSL* ended up becoming the de facto definitive text for the Yogācāra tradition as it would develop in East Asia. In Japan, for instance, works on Yogācāra composed by Japanese masters usually took the *CWSL* as their base text.

In applying a name to the school in East Asia, there was no strong attempt made to maintain the original Sanskrit rubric of Yogācāra, and the main figures of the tradition tended to define it in terms of one of its central, yet difficult to grasp tenets: "consciousness-only" (Ch. *wei shi*)— which paid attention to the central epistemological problem taken up by the school, that nothing in the world can be apprehended apart from one's complex of cognitive processes. The formal name that became attached to the school later on, however, interestingly enough, was originally applied with disparaging intent by members of a rival school. The masters of Huayan Buddhism, one of the major doctrinal rivals of the Consciousness-only school in the early Tang period, had characterized their own system as one which paid attention to the inner nature of phenomena (in Chinese, *fa xing*). In trying to characterize the Weishi school as one which was absorbed in the superficial manifestations of things, they called it the school that pays attention to the "characteristics of phenomena," in Chinese *fa xiang*. The name Faxiang ended up sticking, and the tradition was transmitted to Korea and Japan with this label. Later, it came to be simply taken as the orthodox name for the tradition, without pejorative connotations.

As noted earlier, the Faxiang school in China would eventually die out, submitting first to the competition with the native Chinese doctrinal systems of Tiantai and Huayan, and finally to the more popular practice oriented schools of Pure Land and Chan. But while it died out as a formal school, the remaining schools would end up relying greatly on the concepts and schema that had been developed by Yogācāra, in creating their own doctrinal explanations of such phenomena as karma, rebirth, and the course to liberation.

Yogācāra thought had a deep influence on Korea, where it was assimilated together with other East Asian doctrinal teachings, but it did not endure long in Korea as a distinct school. In Japan, Hossō (the Japanese reading of the Chinese word Faxiang) became one of the major early schools in Nara and Heian period Buddhism, with the Kōfukuji Temple in Nara as its headquarters. Hossō was an active and distinct tradition in Japan long after its influence had waned in China and Korea, with Hossō scholar monks participating in major doctrinal debates with Pure Land and Tendai opponents into the Kamakura period. Eventually, however, the Hossō tradition would end up losing influence in Japan to the Tendai, Nichiren, Zen, and Pure Land schools that advocated the One Vehicle position (discussed in detail in chapter 9 of this book) in regard to the attainment of liberation. Despite its loss of broad influence, the school does still exist, based at the Kōfukuji Temple in Nara, led by the energetic author of this book.

THE DECISION TO TRANSLATE THIS BOOK

When I was first given the opportunity, a few years back, to teach a course on "Buddhist psychology" (a convenient way of teaching Yogācāra in the university curriculum) and I began to investigate what kinds of books were available written in Japanese to be used as course texts, I discovered, rather quickly, around fifteen candidate books that were written as introductions to this topic. In English, of course, there is not yet one full length introduction to Yogācāra. On the whole, the situation is pretty much the same across the board regarding introductions to various schools and Buddhist topics here in Japan, where there is no lack of such introductory texts (although I do have a feeling that it may be precisely due to the image of Yogācāra as being perceived as "difficult" that some scholars feel pressed to write an easy introduction, ending up with the situation where there are perhaps more "introductions to Yogācāra" than there are for any other tradition).

This disparity should not come as such a great surprise, since Japan is, of course, a country with a long-continuing tradition of Buddhist practice *and* Buddhist scholarship. This means that despite the ongoing tendency toward secularization of society, there is still a significant amount of basic background and interest in Buddhist studies among the public to allow a number of Buddhism-centered publishing houses to stay in business. In addition, the greater volume of production of introductory—and more broadly speaking, popular—books on Buddhism in Japan may simply be due to the fact that most of the scholars are themselves Buddhists, whether formally declared or not, and thus feel a certain personal commitment to use their knowledge as a way of spreading accurate dharma.

Writing a good, accessible, introductory book on Yogācāra is not easy—and in some sense, even more difficult for a scholar who has spent his life immersed in Yogācāra studies. Yogācāra material is so complex that those who try to deliver an introduction of this system to the average reader find that it is quite difficult to get started without getting the reader entangled in a morass of arcane complexities. This is unfortunate, since the gist of what Yogācāra has to teach, on a practical level, is rather straightforward, dealing with quite observable and logical matters of everyday experience.

As mentioned above, when I first began to peruse the introductory Yogācāra books available to me in Japanese, I found more than a dozen possible candidates, most of them published by some of the leading authorities in the field. In perusing these texts, however, I found out that almost every single one of them jumped immediately into dense historical and doctrinal issues that would be far beyond the capacities of my undergraduates, none of whom were Buddhist studies majors. These books also did not attempt to explain how one might understand these Yogācāra concepts—especially those concerning the individual function of karma—in terms of one's own lived experience. There was, however, an exception, a book entitled *Hajimete no yuishiki* (Lit. "Beginning Consciousness-only") written by the present abbot of Kōfukuji, Tagawa Shun'ei. I found this book to be well written, offering a concerted effort to try to show how the principles of Yogācāra might be observed, and even applied in the course of one's daily living. Its explanations of the functions of consciousness, while thorough, did not get bogged down in technical language or philological and historical complexities. There was ample use of metaphor and examples to clarify doctrinal explanations.

Thus, I selected it for use in my course. It turned out to be a success, and having read through the book a few years in a row, I began to realize that I would be able to translate it into English without too much difficulty. Aware that there was not yet a comparable work available in English, I undertook the task.

In my translation, I have done my best to be faithful to the original text, but there are places where I have taken the liberty of deleting information (for example, discussions of Japanese *kanji,* or other Japanese cultural materials that I thought to be overly tangential to the discussion). I have also added information (such as some Sanskrit equivalents, and other explanatory background that I thought would be helpful to a Western audience). The largest overall change is seen in my decision to render the ubiquitous Japanese term *yuishiki* as *Yogācāra,* rather than the literal *consciousness-only.* The reason for this decision is that I felt that in the vast majority of cases where the author uses this term, he is referring to a group of thinkers, to a tradition, rather than the specific epistemological position of that tradition.

In East Asia, it is quite common to refer to the tradition as "consciousness-only" (Ch. *weishi;* Kor. *yusik;* Jp. *yuishiki*) but in the West, a significant portion of the scholars who specialize in this tradition do so not from an East Asian background, but from an Indian or Tibetan approach, and within this group, a clear custom has developed to refer to the tradition by its Indian name of Yogācāra. I felt that in order to contribute to the growth of a unified discourse of research and study in the West on this topic, it would be less confusing if East Asianists such as myself also refer to the overall tradition itself by the name of Yogācāra, rather than by the term "consciousness-only." Also, in attempting to use the term consciousness-only, there is already a problem of potentially confusing multiple vocabulary with the various English renderings of *vijñapti-mātratā* and *cittamātra* with such terms as "mind-only," "mere-representation," "cognition-only," "mere cognition," and so on. Hence my decision to stick with *Yogācāra.*

A. Charles Muller
Tokyo, 2009

Foreword

In recent years, Japan has seen a noticeable interest developing in the Indian and post-Indian forms of Buddhism that served as the backdrop for the formation of the Heian and Kamakura Buddhism. The general public has come to understand that there are doctrinal teachings of Buddhism upon which such foundational Japanese masters as Kūkai and Saichō, Shinran, Dōgen, and Nichiren greatly relied in making their own impact on their local form of the tradition. One of these Buddhist doctrinal systems that originates in India is that of Yogācāra Buddhism—commonly referred to in East Asia as "Consciousness-only Buddhism."

The Indian Buddhist schools of Abhidharma and Yogācāra together form a extremely detailed and complex scholarly system. To indicate the difficulties involved in learning these two extremely complex Buddhist doctrinal systems, there is an old saying, "Yogācāra three years, Abhidharma eight years," reflecting the amount of time it is thought to take to truly master these two systems.

Although Yogācāra Buddhism is a notoriously complex doctrinal system, at the same time it is a straightforward and realistic teaching that offers much that we can draw upon for application to our daily lives. However, due to its complexity, truly accessible introductory works written on the topic have been few and far between: detailed complexity and simplicity don't go so well with each other.

Despite the difficulties to be seen in putting together a good introductory work on Yogācāra, Japanese specialists in this area have made efforts to compose and publish some relatively easy introductory works for public consumption, which has in turn led to an increase in interest on the part of general readers. Nonetheless, we still often hear complaints from readers that these books are too difficult, and it is thus in response to these voices that I have endeavored to write a book that avoids discussion of hair-splitting details, and which, in as simple a language as possible, provides an introductory account of the basic Yogācāra teachings.

While Yogācāra may on one hand be characterized as nothing more than the extended study of basic Buddhist doctrine, it is also something that is complete as a single religious system in itself. Therefore, in teaching about Yogācāra, it is not merely my intention to select a list of essential items and explain how these are experienced in the course of living one's daily living. Rather, it is my intention to explain the religious significance of these teachings, and exactly how, as a whole, they can be appropriated and applied in our daily lives.

This does not mean that this is the only way the book is to be read—I think that this is something that needs to be tried and tested by each reader from his own standpoint. One should be able to gain personal access to the Yogācāra teachings while at the same time apply these within the framework of understanding Buddhism that one has developed heretofore. If this book can in any way help to facilitate such an approach, I will be very grateful.

Tagawa Shun'ei
March 6, 1989

Chapter One: Yogācāra Is...

NOTHING BUT THE TRANSFORMATIONS OF CONSCIOUSNESS

> I built my hut amid the throng of men,
> But there is no din of carriages or horses.
> You ask me how this can be?
> When the heart is remote, the earth stands aloof.
> Plucking chrysanthemums by the eastern hedge,
> I see afar the southern hills;
> The mountain air is fine at sunset;
> Flying birds return home in flocks.
> In this return lies real meaning;
> I want to explain it, but I lose the words.
>   Tao Yuanming, "Drinking Wine"

It might be surprising that I choose to open up this discussion with Tao Yuanming's poem "Drinking Wine."[1] However, seeing that we are going to engage ourselves with Yogācāra Buddhism from the perspective of its relevance in dealing with our daily lives, I would like to take this poem as our point of departure.

I was in my second year of high school when I was first introduced to this Chinese poem. Since that time, I have continued to re-read it from time to time, and whenever I do, a proverb comes to mind, which goes: "The great recluse hides himself in the city markets; the minor recluse hides in the deep mountains." Our teacher, Mr. U., also taught us this proverb for the purpose of drawing out the meaning of the poem. I remember having been somewhat puzzled by its meaning at the time, but later on, after entering into the world of Buddhism, its meaning became increasingly clear.

While it is indeed the case that anyone who is practicing meditation in a Buddha-hall is seeking enlightenment as some sort of distant goal, the fact is that the temples, practice centers, and the Buddhist path do not exist for any purpose other than for us to fully understand ourselves exactly as we are here and now. Where we are now, as shown in Tao Yuanming's poem—the hut in the midst of the world of people—is precisely our practice center, and so it doesn't do us any good to try to escape from it. We should think about the Buddha-path and the meditation hall in the way of the great recluse who "withdraws to the city streets." This is the main reason this poem resonates with me, and thus I continue to re-read it.

But there is also another reason.

Tao Yuanming has told us that in the noisy world of men—living in the middle of the city—he hears no noisy traffic. He has, in answering his own question, arrived at a conclusion: "when the mind is remote, the earth stands aloof." I take "When the mind is remote" to mean that the mind is distantly removed from its attachments. So what is this world of ours, when viewed by the person who has a "remote mind"? Whether it be someone who boisterously takes the lead in worldly affairs, or, on the other hand, the spiritually-attuned person who is profoundly aware of the pitfalls of deep attachment to one's ego—both of these people are, after all, overwhelmed by, and washed along in the flow of daily affairs. However, we can be certain that they are perceiving their circumstances along the way in a quite different manner.

The great recluse Tao Yuanming tells us that he is removed from the clamor of the world of men. But how about us? We ordinary people frequently seek to be able to escape from day-to-day living in the way of the lesser recluse, who goes deep in the mountains to be alone. If we really think it through, we can say that while we live in the same world, each person sees things in his or her own way, and there is a sense in which each one of us is in fact living in his own world. This fact is very interesting to take into account as we accumulate the experiences of daily living, yet from another perspective, it can also be a bit scary.

Given the admonition of Tao Yuanming about "distancing the mind," what we need to consider is whether such "distancing" is actually a function of our own minds, and if so, if it is a fundamental, innate function—or perhaps even the mind's basic character? The Yogācāra teachings that we will discuss constitute the form of Buddhism that has taken under the deepest consideration these problems regarding the composition and function of our mind.

The Yogācāra project, which attempts to accurately map out the concrete structure of our minds, develops as the result of coming to a profound understanding of the relationship between ourselves and the myriad objects in our environment, and then correlating these with the basic teachings of Śākyamuni Buddha. The central tenet of Yogācāra is usually said to be that of "consciousness-only," which means, more precisely, "nothing but the transformations of consciousness."

The characterization "nothing but the transformations of consciousness" can be further as "nothing but that which has been transformed by consciousness." I am afraid, however, that starting off with this kind of arcane approach is probably not very helpful for newcomers to this topic, so I'd like to step back and take a gentler approach for a moment.

> At the clapping of hands,
> The carp come swimming for food;
> The birds fly away in fright, and
> A maiden comes carrying tea—
> Sarusawa Pond.

This is a line of Japanese *tanka* poetry, which expresses distinct ways of interpreting a particular event, based on a few traditional Japanese images. If one claps one's hands the carp (which are conditioned to come for feeding at the clap of the hands) will come swimming to the water's edge for food; birds, on the other hand, will fly away in fright. Yet again, to the waitress in the traveler's inn, it is a notification that the guest wants tea.

Sarusawa Pond (Monkey Marsh Pond) lies in the middle of a famous tourist area in Nara. It is said that this verse was written because there are so many travelers inns *(ryokan)* in that area, but it is also well known as a

place where one can, from the water's edge, look up at the impressing figure of the five-story pagoda of Kōfukuji temple.

Yogācāra is the doctrine of the Hossō (Ch. Faxiang) school, one of the
six schools of the southern (Nara) court, and Kōfukuji is the long-
flourishing headquarters for the study of Hossō teachings. Therefore, this
tanka line which at first glance does not appear to say anything out of the
ordinary, actually is a direct expression of the essence of the Yogācāra way
of thinking.

The subject of the verse is the extremely simple action of "clapping the
hands." This verse shows that despite the singular character of this action,
and the singular character of the sound that is generated, its meaning can
be dramatically different depending upon the individual conditions of the
receiver of the sound.

On the other hand, we can all call to mind the case of seeing the same
thing many times over and over. Everyone has had the experience of having their impression of a particular object change depending upon their
feelings or conditions at a given moment. This is because the object is seen
under the influence of the mental state of that moment. Of course, at the
time when we are looking at something, we are generally not aware of the
way our feelings are being projected into the situation.

Seen in this way, our so-called cognition, or the action of discerning the
meaning of things as they are perceived by us, is never in any case a perception of the external world exactly as it is, but rather a world that can only
be apprehended via its interface with our present mental state. In other
words, it is nothing other than our own mind that constructs things and
determines their content. This is the meaning of "consciousness-only," or
"nothing but the transformations of consciousness." And, if we turn this
around, we ourselves are nothing other than things that dwell in a world
defined by the limits of that which is knowable by the functions of our
own mind.

There is a sense in which this can actually seem pretty scary. Why?
Because if there is abundance in my mind, I'll be able to experience life
dwelling in a world of abundance; but on the other hand, if there is poverty
in my mind, there will be no recourse except for me to reside in a world of
poverty. If I have no recourse but to finish my days in poverty, this would

indeed be a sad human limitation. However, the notion of "nothing but the transformations of consciousness" teaches us accurately about the mode of the reality we experience. Because of this, we can develop a deep awareness that we have no recourse but to continually and repeatedly reflect on ourselves. The effort of trying to live life with this kind of earnest reflection can be understood to be the practice of Yogācāra Buddhism.

THE FOUR ASPECTS OF COGNITION AND THE THREE KINDS OF OBJECTS

As we have broached the topic of *consciousness-only* and *nothing but the transformations of consciousness* through this poetic imagery, I would like to proceed by providing a few further examples from daily experience that will hopefully shed further light on these notions.

We are, in the midst of our day-to-day affairs, continuously experiencing the mental functions of seeing, hearing, and thinking, assuming all the while that we are directly seeing, hearing, and understanding the external world. But careful analysis makes it quite clear that this cannot actually be the case. According to Yogācāra Buddhism, what we actually perceive are *images* of the things of the external world as they are *transformed by our own consciousness,* and reflected onto our own mind. This being so, the things of the world that we are seeing and hearing cannot be the world exactly as it is. All of the things around us are the transformations by our own consciousnesses. This is the basic Yogācāra approach to understanding the relationship between ourselves and our environment.

We assume that we are sensing and seeing the scenery of the mountains in the distance and clouds in the sky that spread out before us in the way that these things actually exist. We also prefer to think that we are accurately recognizing the people and events surrounding us as we carry out our daily lives. When someone happens to point out that our view lacks objectivity and is off the mark, we don't like it.

However, if we think it through, even though the mountain we are presently seeing is a single entity, upon reflection it should become clear to us that we are actually seeing the mountain via the medium of the outward-going projection of various mental conditions that are specific to us as individuals. Rather than seeing the mountain as it really is, what I am actually seeing is a mountain that is colored and altered by my own mind.

It is said that a painter picks up the brush upon the feeling of being moved by the power of the scene of the mountain that stands before him. When we look at the scenes of Mt. Fuji painted by famous Japanese artists such as Hayashitake and Ryuzaburo Umehara, even though theoretically speaking we should see in their respective works the same exact image of the mountain, the Mt. Fuji that ends up being painted on the canvas contains a wide range of distortions.

Concerning this, Nakagawa Kazumasa (a famous living Japanese artist) has written that the work of the painter is to "fix" what is moved in his mind, while the mind that receives this deep impression "undoes" the shape. If this is the case, then we can say that the distorted image of Mt. Fuji that is painted onto the canvas is one that has been transformed in the painter's mind according to the received impression, and this is what the painter has fixated upon.

Although these kinds of artistic distortions may not be readily apparent while we are in the process of carrying out our daily lives, it is nonetheless the case that while we are in the midst of our daily activities, we are, just like these painters, perceiving all the things we must come in contact with differently according to our various mental states. And we can take it a step further and say that we are also transforming and perceiving things in the way that provides the greatest *convenience* for the carrying out of our life. According to Yogācāra, this is a stark fact of our existence.

Because our mind is actually working like an agent that manifests all objects of cognition, the Yogācāras, rather than simply calling it "mind," call it "the mind that transforms" or "the mind as agent of transformation." In the same vein, because our cognitive objects (or "objective realm") are things that are in fact manifested by the mind-as-agent-of-transformation, they are called "transformed objects," rather than simply "objects."

To explain the functions of the subjectively transforming mind and objectively transformed objects in a coherent system, Yogācāra developed the teaching of the *four aspects of cognition* and the *three kinds of objects*. The explanation of the four aspects of cognition clarifies the function of the mind in its role as transforming subject, and the explanation of the three kinds of objects clarifies the character of the objects that are transformed. Within these theories, the Yogācāras carry out a hair-splitting analysis in regard to our cognitive functioning. This kind of subtle analysis is a bit hard to get the first time around, but efforts made toward understanding it are truly worthwhile, since once one has gotten this, it can be said that one has penetrated the core principle of Yogācāra. Therefore the saying, "if one understands the four aspects of cognition and three kinds of objects, the mastery of Yogācāra is half accomplished."

The Four Aspects of Cognition

The theory of the four aspects of cognition, which clarifies the action of the "mind that acts as agent of transformation" tells us that the processes of our cognitive function can be divided into four parts. These are: (1) the objective aspect; (2) subjective aspect; (3) witnessing aspect; and (4) re-witnessing aspect.

In the process of the cognition of any given object, the first step is the mental function of perceiving the object and then determining what it is. In general, it is understood that this is an *external object* (something outside the mind). It is normally assumed that this thing that is "outside the mind" is taken as object, and the mind subjectively identifies it. So most of us think.

However, according to Yogācāra, when the cognitive mental functioning is activated, the mind itself is actually divided into four aspects, depending upon the particular function, and that which we know as cognitive function is established based on this division. These four are the aspects of: (1) that which is seen (objective aspect), (2) that which sees (subjective aspect); (3) the confirmation of that seeing (witnessing aspect), and (4) the acknowledgment of that confirmation (re-witnessing aspect). Usually, even in the case when we are firmly convinced that we are directly perceiving and understanding something that exists outside of the mind, the fact is that it is actually this *objective aspect* that has been transformed within our minds. In other words, although that which appears in our minds is nothing more than an image resembling that object, we take it to be the actual object of our cognition.

If this is indeed the case, one might well extend this point further to say that what we call cognition is nothing but "the mind seeing the mind." It would certainly not be wrong to say this, but it is not that simple, either. This will be covered fully below. The analysis of these four aspects, especially the notion of the objective aspect that is transformed from its original form in being taken as an object of the mind, and being thought of as an image, originates in the Yogācāra school, as the word *yogācāra* ("yoga practice") refers to the practice of focusing one's mind—meditative concentration.

In the commonsense understanding of the notion, the idea of focusing one's mind in meditation is usually associated with the severing of the connection with the external world, assuring that, in the state of deep meditation, there is little connection with concrete things. However, it was often the case that adepts at yoga practice had the experience of seeing an image of the Buddha as the content of their deep meditation. Of course, that Buddha was a Buddha seen from the individual meditator's own perspective, and so there was no such thing as a physically present Buddha corresponding directly to this image.

Based on this experience, Yogācāra practitioners came to the conclusion that the cognitive object called "Buddha" was something that was manifested from within their own minds. As they gradually came to an understanding of the function of the mind that confirmed that what they were seeing in meditation was in fact the Buddha (rather than something, or someone, else *other* than the Buddha), they eventually arrived to the establishment of the doctrine of the four aspects of cognition.

The doctrine of the four aspects of cognition takes as its objects both the cognition of sensory objects in our daily life as well as those things that are manifested by our mind. Taking this as a focal point, and reflecting again upon the commonly-held assumption that we see things as they actually are, we come to gain a modicum of understanding of the fact that these things are never seen in any way *except that which is suitable to us.* To the extent that our mental functioning is subject to this limitation, there is no reason to assume that we will ever see anything as it actually is. Thus the characterization as "nothing but the transformations of consciousness" strongly suggests that our assumption that we see things as they actually exist is in need of serious reconsideration.

This demarcation of these cognitive functions into these four parts of cognitive function of objective aspect, subjective aspect, witnessing aspect, and re-witnessing aspect is usually difficult to grasp the first time around. For the purpose of aiding in the understanding of this process, a simile based on the process of measuring cloth has long been used. In it, the cloth represents the objective aspect, with the subjective aspect being the measuring scale. The witnessing aspect is seen as the function of coming to know the size of the cloth, and the re-witnessing aspect is represented by the notation of the size of the cloth.

Another way of thinking about the four aspects can be seen in the case where at the moment I say, "I am presently looking at my watch, and the time is 7:30 pm." In that situation, first, the watch is the objective aspect, and the seeing of the watch is the subjective aspect. Then, the confirmation of the fact that the hands of the clock are indicating the position of 7:30 is like the witnessing aspect. Then, since it is usually the case that when that kind of confirmation is made, it is something done consciously, this kind of conscious stage can be understood to be the re-witnessing aspect.

Three Categories of Transformed Objects

Three categories are utilized in order to clarify the character of objects that are transformed: (1) objects as they are in themselves—their raw sensate appearance; (2) objects that are merely illusion, and (3) objects that are originally derived from raw sensate appearance but which end up being falsely perceived. Here, I would just like to introduce these concepts without going into extensive detail. But the reader should understand that this category of "objects of cognition" under discussion here is none other than the objective aspect (discussed just above) that manifests through transformation in the mind. Here, the three categories are distinguished in terms of the extent to which they are grounded in raw sensate experience (for the sake of simplicity, let's just say "the actual things of the external world"):

(1) The objects as they are in themselves are images manifested through transformation based on raw sensate appearance, and are correct objects of cognition.

(2) On the other hand, the objects that are completely illusory have no relationship to the raw sensate appearance, but are images projected on the mind by the power of the attention that the mind has generated on its own, and thus are utterly ungrounded cognitive objects. Illusions are good examples of the objects of this category.

(3) Things that "derive from raw sensate appearance but which are mistakenly perceived" are objects that despite being grounded in raw sensate appearance are, due to the circumstances, not correctly apprehensible, and thus they are the sorts of objects that we call "mistaken," "misconstrued," or "misidentified."

We touch upon various things every day, meet various kinds of people, and are encountering various situations and events as we carry out our day-to-day living. At that time, is quite natural for us to think that in regard to the objects of our mental functions of perceiving, thinking, and making judgments, that we are directly seeing, hearing, and making judgments in regard to this and that object. However, according to Yogācāra Buddhism, those cognized objects have already been colored and transformed by our minds in the process of their manifestation.

There are those who would object by saying it is the environment that determines the mental consciousness. However, the relationship between oneself and the things that surround oneself is not that simple. As we have already seen, it is more the case that one's mind determines the content of the environment, and that "self" surrounded by the environment which was secretly manifested through transformation is once again cognized by us. This is understood as the real composition of things.

Despite the lack of any evidence to support this case, we tend to feel rather stubbornly that our own view of things is undistorted. But with a thorough pursuit of the Yogācāra way of thinking, this problematic sense of infallibility is readily dissolved.

Chapter Two: The Structure of the Mind

SURFACE MIND AND DEEP MIND

We lead our lives surrounded by all sorts of things. When annoyed, we may try to escape them by moving to the quiet and simple life in the middle of the mountains, but the fact of our being surrounded by many things does not change at all. As long as we are alive, there is no way that we can ever sever ourselves from our environment. In managing our daily lives, we have no recourse but to proceed while maintaining some kind of relationship with all those things that surround us. At such a time, there will always be things, people, and events. Rather than seeking to escape from them, what we need to do is examine the way we cognize these things, and the way we understand their content.

In Yogācāra Buddhism, unusually deep consideration was undertaken in regard to the nature of cognitive function and the objects of cognition. As a result of their investigations, Yogācāra thinkers came to the conclusion that although as a matter of convention we perceive the things of the external world as if they were directly apprehended by us, and although we furthermore think that we correctly interpret their meaning based on this direct apprehension, these objects do not in fact exist in this way. Rather, the Yogācārins said that these cognitive objects are actually transformed by our own minds, and then are reflected onto our minds as *images that resemble those things.*

Since an image that resembles the thing is conjured through transformation and floated on the mind, it is natural that some of its distinctive aspects will be sufficiently transmitted such that we can recognize it. However, we have good reason to doubt the extent to which this manifestation actually reflects the appearance of the thing as it is. Despite this reasonable suspicion, we proceed along with our lives thinking that we are accurately seeing, hearing, judging, and understanding the objects that impinge on our awareness. Since none of us are intentionally trying to change the appearance of these objects, wanting to distort their shape, or alter their appearance, we unthinkingly live out our lives believing that we are cognizing everything accurately.

An important implication of coming to terms with this observation is that our daily life is not lived only in the mental domains of conscious awareness. The regions of mind which we can reflect on and regulate are known in Buddhism as the six consciousnesses: the visual consciousness, auditory consciousness, olfactory consciousness, gustatory consciousness, tactile consciousness, and thinking consciousness. However, these six kinds of awareness alone cannot account for the full range of our thoughts and activities. For example, standing in front of the same mountain, the seasoned veteran mountain climber and the raw novice see the face of that mountain with a dramatically different understanding. Our ordinary thinking consciousness has accumulated a great number of years' experience, for which it lacks the capacity to contain fully.

It was in regard to this observation that the Yogācārins, deliberating on the composition of our mind and its functions of conscious awareness, came to be convinced that there had to be an additional, deeper layer of mind, which, while continuously imposing its influence on everyday conscious awareness, also served as its underlying basis. Thus, they posited a subconscious region of the mind, comprised of the two deep layers of consciousness of *manas* and *ālaya-vijñāna*.

The custom of numbering the major distinct faculties of consciousnesses was in place from the time of early Indian Buddhism, and was still retained as a basic standard in the lesser vehicle Buddhism taught in texts such as the *Abhidharmakośa-bhāsya*. Yogācāra Buddhism, in its earliest stages, took this traditional scheme as its point of departure, but its thinkers gradually began to develop their own distinct model, having come to the conclusion that these six could not account for the entire mind, and represented nothing more than its surface aspect.

Within these six consciousnesses, the visual, auditory, olfactory, gustatory, and tactile consciousnesses each operate specifically in response to colors and shapes, sounds, odors, tastes, and tactile objects. They correspond to what we know as sight, hearing, sense of smell, taste, and sense of touch—in other words, the five senses, each sensory activity occurring through its corresponding sense organ. These five consciousnesses all share the feature of only being able to cognize a presently existing object as it is.

For example, in the case where the visual consciousness arises based on the presence of a red flower, the material object that constitutes the objective aspect of the visual consciousness is nothing more than the direct perception of a red-hued object with a certain shape. At this point, it is a type of cognition which lacks any intermediary, such as language, to apply meaning. This is what we call direct perception. At this stage, there is no understanding that says, "This is a bright red flower, and this flower is a lotus." The object of cognition at this time is an object as it is in itself—a raw sensate appearance among the three kinds of objects described in chapter 1. Since the lotus flower has an incredible fragrance, the olfactory consciousness naturally arises, creating a scent that is known exclusively by the olfactory consciousness.

The cognition that "this is a bright red flower, this flower is a lotus, and it has a very good smell" is something that occurs on the next level, that of the function of the thinking consciousness *(mano-vijñāna)*. The thinking consciousness, the sixth, accounts for the mental functions of perception, emotion, deliberation, and volition, and is essentially equivalent to what is referred to as "the mind" in everyday language. Expressing this with the present-day idiom of "information processor," the information gathered is that which is perceived by the five consciousnesses, gathered through the five sense faculties.

The method of processing this information is a problem of the function of the thinking consciousness. The five consciousnesses of eyes, ears, noses, tongue, and body all constitute relatively simple cognitive functions. Since these consciousnesses are understood to operate "prior" to the thinking consciousness, they are usually subsumed as a group under the rubric of *prior five consciousnesses*.

The sixth, thinking consciousness, functions concurrently with the prior five consciousnesses. Taking the pure cognition of the object as it is, and recognizing that "this is a bright red lotus flower, which has a wonderful fragrance" is the function of the thinking consciousness. While the prior five consciousnesses are limited in only being able to directly perceive a presently existent object as it is, the sixth thinking consciousness, while functioning in the framework of the present, can also reflect back upon the past as well as anticipate the future.

Since the cognition of present objects by the prior five consciousnesses just as they are occurs through the sense organs, a temporary interruption (such as when one shuts one's eyes) will lead the cognitive function of that consciousness to be terminated. While the cognition by the prior five consciousnesses is limited to a particular place—the thinking consciousness— the mental activity concerning the lotus flower that has been seen up until then can be continued. It is precisely because of this ability to maintain continuity that one may reflect afterward on the lotus flower repeatedly and from various perspectives, giving one's imagination free reign. Recollecting the past, anticipating the future, or carrying out a variety of calculations and comparisons, and then gathering and synthesizing all of these—these are the functions of the thinking consciousness.

In considering the prior five consciousnesses and the thinking consciousness, we can easily imagine the numerous differences in terms of the range of their function, or the objective referent that they discern. Nonetheless, since the prior five consciousnesses and the sixth consciousness share in common the general function of discerning and distinguishing the content of their respective objects, Yogācāra Buddhism categorizes the prior five and the thinking consciousness together as the *consciousnesses that discern objects*. However, for Yogācāra these six consciousnesses are far from being all there is to the mind, since these object-discerning consciousnesses do not suffice to explain the full gamut of our mental life.

THE ĀLAYA-VIJÑĀNA AND THE MANAS

1. The Limitations of the Six Consciousnesses

As distinguished from the view of the six consciousnesses in place since early Indian Buddhism, the Yogācāras hypothesized that our mind was composed of eight consciousnesses. The eight consciousnesses include the six object-discerning consciousnesses, plus the *manas* (fundamental mentation consciousnesses), and *ālaya-vijñāna* (store consciousness).

If we attempt earnestly to ascertain the true aspect of our human existence—to whatever degree it is knowable—we must assume that there is a subconscious mind that, while serving as the basis for our existence, is ceaselessly exerting great influence on our conscious daily lives. It is precisely the proof and definition of this subconscious mind that the Yogācāras took up as their central focus of their investigations. Above, we explained that the accumulation of long years of experience is something that cannot be accounted for within the function of the thinking consciousness. To test this, let's reflect on our own past for a moment.

Despite its vast range of function beyond that of the sense consciousnesses, if we consider the sixth consciousness from the perspective of the full range of our past experiences, it turns out to be something quite shallow and limited. Obviously, we forget many of the things we have done over our lifetimes. However, imagine if there were no retention whatsoever of the traces of those events that have occurred within ourselves? If this were the case, no matter what we might apply ourselves to do, it would be impossible for us to improve at anything. However, we know that with even a small amount of practice, we are going to become better and more skilled. For the time being, then, we have to acknowledge that there has to be a mental region where such experiences are accurately retained. But what becomes of the thinking consciousness when we are sleeping soundly? Since its mode of existence is thinking, and thinking has ceased, practically speaking, that consciousness has ceased to exist. There is a complete interruption in the function and existence of this consciousness. This notion of interruption is critical in the Yogācāra theory of the mind.

The thinking consciousness is not something that is operating continuously—it has intervals. This is something that is readily understandable in commonsense terms, but there is a special problem in this fact for Buddhism, since unlike other religions that assume the existence of an enduring soul, or self *(ātman)* that grounds the being and holds it together in times of mental inactivity, one of the basic tenets of the Buddhist teaching is that any such assumed self cannot be anything other than a fiction.

This being the case, there is nothing to unite these interruptions, and even a provisional self as a unifying entity cannot be posited. Having come to this conclusion, they decided that there has to be a latent area of the mind that is uninterrupted, firmly retaining the aftereffects of all we have done. Yogācāra Buddhism argued for the existence of such a mind, and called it *ālaya-vijñāna* (store consciousness).

2. The Ālaya-Vijñāna and the Manas

In Yogācāra, the mind called the *ālaya-vijñāna* is hypothesized to be the most fundamental mind, the mental region that accounts for the unbroken continuity extending from the past to the future.

Practically speaking, there has to be an "I" that is changing on a daily basis. But we know from experience that the I of yesterday is virtually the same as the I of today, and there is not so much difference between the I of a year ago and the I of today. We naturally feel like this. This changing-but-unchanging so-called self is what we take to be our basis, that upon which the stability of our life is maintained. And that basis is the *ālaya-vijñāna*.

In a Buddhist framework, although we say "changing yet unchanging self," we are not talking about an unchanging essence, but something that is fundamentally impermanent in its nature. We nonetheless end up grasping this aspect of continuity and misconstrue it to be an unchanging, reified self. It is said that in addition to the *ālaya-vijñāna,* we also have within us an aspect of mentation that is carrying out this "I-making" function. The Yogācāras first posited this aspect of mind, which they called the *manas,* proposing that there is a function of mind that is secretly, ceaselessly attaching itself to the notion of a continuous and unbroken self. Since the *manas* is also engaged in a rudimentary kind of thought, some of its functions also overlap with those of the thinking consciousness.

It was already stated that the task of gathering and determining how to process information was one of the functions of the thinking consciousness. But it is unlikely that the thinking consciousness would be capable of fully operating in an independent manner during this information processing. Concerning this, Yogācāra hypothesizes that the thinking consciousness has the *manas* as its support (Skt. *āśraya*).

The "I-making" function of the *manas* also has an outward-going influence, since Yogācāra Buddhism understands that no matter how accurate a judgment we endeavor to make, we are essentially incapable of going beyond the purview of a judgment that we believe would be good for our own situation. This is taken as evidence of the pervasive and unbroken function of the *manas*. The *manas* in turn takes the *ālaya-vijñāna* as its underlying basis. Thus, in Yogācāra Buddhism the *ālaya-vijñāna* is understood to be the most basic form of mind.

3. The Three Subjective Transformations

Thus, the Yogācāras began to conjecture the structure of mind as being composed of eight consciousnesses, distributed in two deep levels of mind as the *manas* and *ālaya-vijñāna,* followed by the six surface levels including the visual, auditory, olfactory, gustatory, tactile, and thinking consciousnesses. As we have also noted, our mind has the function of manifesting the object of cognition on the mind as an "image." In this very important sense, the mind is not simply seen as mind, but as a mind that carries out transformations. This *mind as subjective transformer* consists of three layers.

The first mind as subjective transformer is the *ālaya-vijñāna.* The *ālaya-vijñāna* flawlessly retains all of our past experiences, and recognizes and contextualizes things as we cognize them. Our experiences, according to their depth and significance upon our lives, are difficult to remove.

The second subjective transformer is the *manas.* In this case, objects of cognition are transformed by a deep attachment to the self, and the resulting tendencies to protect and further that self.

Then, already subject to these subconscious influences, the cognitive function of the thinking consciousness and the five sense consciousnesses—that is, the discrimination of things—arises. When one is focused on seeing or hearing, what is seen and what is heard are naturally different from each other. Since these consciousnesses are aware only of their own objects, the only things that are transformed are their own objective images. Thus, the six object-aware consciousnesses together constitute the third subjective transformer.

From this we can begin to understand the profound difficulties involved in knowing the actual way of being of any given thing as it really is.

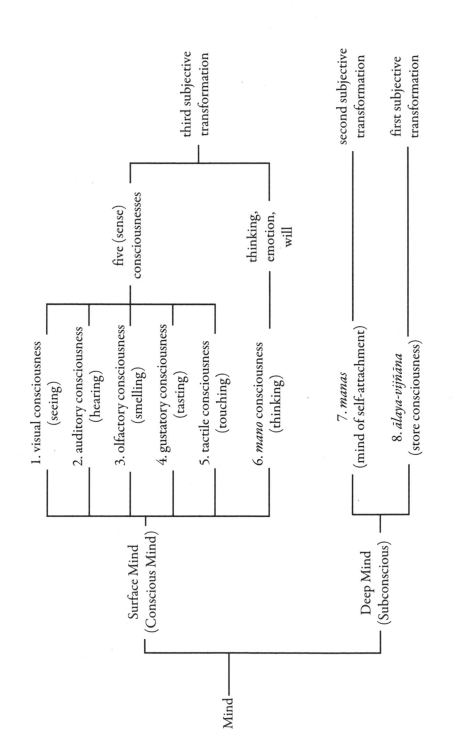

Chapter Three: The Functions of the Mind

THE MIND-KING AND MENTAL FUNCTIONS

In the course of our everyday lives, we casually refer to the psychological aspect of our existence as *mind* without giving it special thought. Yogācāra Buddhists saw the mind as being distinguishable into eight kinds of aspects (eight consciousnesses), and furthermore saw them as dynamically constituting the three subjective transformations.

In East Asian Yogācāra Buddhism, the eight consciousnesses are known collectively as the *eight consciousnesses mind-king (citta)*. While mind is usually regarded as a single entity, when it is analyzed into its substance and its functions, the term mind-king is used to connote the sense of "master," or "main part." In contrast to this are the functions that occur based within this substantive mind-king, which are called *mental factors* (Skt. *caitta*).

In Yogācāra, the essence of the substantive mind-king is first understood to cognize the essential, or general aspects of things, after which it gives rise to discriminating, discursive knowing. The mind-king-as-substance first executes a general type of cognition, and as it begins its activity, the mental functions arise and begin to scrutinize the object in greater detail, at the same time generating various thoughts.

For instance, when we are presented with a blue box, the general recognition that it is a blue box is made by the mind-king. After that, the detailed cognition that the main part of the box is deep blue, and the lid only is light blue, is the work of mental factors. And of course, the further thought that "I want this box" also occurs within the mental factors. Whether it is a thing, a person, or an event, according to Yogācāra we are completing our cognitive function through this process.

Yogācāra posits fifty-one of these mental factors, which are categorized into six general types. As explained in the *Lucid Introduction to the One Hundred Dharmas,*[2] they are arranged in this manner:

(1) *omnipresent factors:* attention, contact, sensation, perception, intention.

(2) *object-contingent factors:* desire, resolve, mindfulness, concentration, intelligence.

(3) *wholesome factors:* faith, zeal, conscience, shame, not coveting, no anger, no folly, pliancy, no laxity, indifference, not harming.

(4) *afflictions:* craving, ill-will, pride, ignorance, doubt, incorrect views.

(5) *secondary afflictions:* anger, enmity, anxiety, concealing, deceit, flattery, arrogance, hostility, jealousy, parsimony, unscrupulousness, shamelessness, unbelief, indolence, negligence, slackness, agitation, forgetting, incorrect cognition, distraction.

(6) *four uncategorized factors:* drowsiness, regret, discovery, scrutiny.

These technical terms for our mental functions were developed as the result of the work of a long tradition of Buddhist scholasticism examining human behavior, and precisely identifying the variety of modes of our mental functioning in daily life. This terminology was further developed into its final form by the Yogācāra school.

For instance, the wholesome group consists of good mental functions that improve one's spiritual condition. Basic Buddhist teachings state that if we continually maintain these kinds of mental functions, we will eventually arrive to the states of a buddha or bodhisattva. Conversely, the mental functions that bring unremitting suffering to our bodies and minds are listed in the category containing the twenty-six items of the *afflictions* and *secondary afflictions.*

These mental factors are concrete mental functions that we all experience. The clear presentation of the concrete functions of the mind are just the first indication of the precision with which Yogācāra Buddhism attempts to scrutinize the actual condition of the human mind. It is a view of humanity that, while focusing on human behavior as the intersection of goodness and affliction, tries to realize suffering, regardless of its depth. Yogācāra also tells us that it is precisely within the subtle intertwining of these mental functions that that intense suffering is brought to body and mind, and only based on sincere reflection in the course of our everyday living can the religious world be established.

Since we will be taking up the wholesome factors, the afflictions, and secondary afflictions categories for detailed examination in chapter 6 and chapter 7, I will here treat the groups of omnipresent, object-contingent, and uncategorized.

OMNIPRESENT AND OBJECT-CONTINGENT FACTORS

1. Omnipresent Factors

Omnipresent factors are the most basic psychological functions active in all situations, concomitant with the mind-king and all mental factors. The five omnipresent factors include: attention, contact, sensation, perception, and volition.

No matter the situation, for cognition to be established, the mind must first be awakened and arouse concern for the object. Attention (Skt. *manaskāra*) is the name of the function of arousing concern for an object, the function that initially stimulates the mind. Once the stimulated mind has come into association with its object, the conditions for establishing cognition are gradually established. Contact (Skt. *sparśa*) puts the mind into such a state, and is the support for the ensuing functions of sensation, perception, and volition.

A problem now arises: In its relation to "me," is the cognitive object that is being taken in something good, something bad, or neither? The reception of the cognitive object is called the mental function of sensation (Skt. *vedanā*). In the case where the object brings about displeasure or pain, it is called *sensation of pain*. Pleasurable sensations are called *sensation of pleasure* and experiences of objects that are neither pleasurable nor painful are called *sensation of indifference*. These are classified together as the three sensations.

Within the process of cognizing an object, our mind becomes entwined in the sensory awareness of liking and disliking at a very early juncture. And since there is such thing as indifferent sensation, we know that not every instance of perception of objects is involved with affectivity. There are numerous objects that we experience in our daily lives that do not result in pleasant/ unpleasant, painful/satisfying sensations and emotions. For instance, we can consider the way reception of cognitive objects is changed when such objects overwhelm us by exceeding our present cognitive capacity.

Perception can be understood as the process of taking in a copy of an image of something into the mind and associating it with words. This mental factor functions in such a way that it takes that thing received as the object of cognition and fits it into the framework possessed by the "I" who receives it. It is at that time that one clearly apprehends exactly what the cognized object is.

Each person has their own frame for apprehending things as a matter of necessity. Yet while an individual's own framework might be unique, each one is deeply influenced by one's society, race, and culture. Why? Because the ultimate frame of perception is none other than language itself. This reception is described as being carried out at the level of the sixth consciousness, meaning that that which is actually digesting information is none other than the framework known as language.

However, speaking of this frame presents another type of restriction, and whether or not the distinct cognition formed upon the basis of language is a valid cognition is another problem. The function of further clarifying the object of cognition by applying language skillfully is understood to be a problem that appears not at this present stage of perception, but rather falls under the purview of the mental factors known as *discovery* (*vitarka*) and *scrutiny* (*vicāra*), which are among the uncategorized factors that will be discussed below. The image of the thing that is to be cognized is clearly copied onto the mind, where it is absorbed. Perception then occurs as the mental function that fits it into one's own behavioral and thought patterning.

The mental factor of volition is understood to be comprised of three sequential stages: (1) evaluation, (2) decision-making, and (3) initiation of action. Evaluation is the basic psychological function taken in regard to the cognition of an object based on the prior phases of attention, contact, sensation, and perception, where the various options involved regarding the taking of action (karma) are contemplated in regard to the object. Decision-making is a mental function wherein one decides whether or not to take a certain type of action in regard to the object. Initiation of action is a mental activity of receiving the content of the decision, and initiating a concrete action.

As for concrete action, our daily activities are completed through three general modes: bodily activity (deeds), verbal activity (speech), and mental activity (thought). *Bodily activity (kāya-karman)* is any action in which bodily function is included, *verbal activity (vāk-karman)* refers to linguistic behavior, and *mental activity (manas-karman)* is the deliberation that occurs in the mind. Mental activity is also understood in a positive sense in Buddhism as the mysterious activity that occurs within our own minds that is inaccessible to others.

Because volition is the mental function that constitutes the mainspring of our concrete behavior, the essences of the three karmas of deed, speech, and thought are to be found within these three stages of volition. The karmas of deed and speech have initiation of action as their essence, and mental activity (thought) has evaluation and decision-making as its essence.

2. Object-Contingent Factors

Object-contingent mental factors differ from the prior omnipresent factors in that they function only in regard to specific objects rather than being operative in every situation. The five object-contingent mental factors include *desire, devoted interest, mindfulness, concentration,* and *intelligence.*

Concerning the karmic moral quality of the objects of these object-dependent factors, it is assumed that these five are not directly associated with either wholesomeness, unwholesomeness, or indeterminacy. While this is similar to the case of the omnipresent factors, object-dependent factors tend to be explained with a focus on wholesome mental functioning. This is the way Yogācāra Buddhism schematizes the mind, but it must be remembered that in the final analysis, the ultimate goal lies in nothing other than entry into Buddha-mind.

Desire (chanda) is a mental function wherein one sees an object for which it holds interest and concern, and hopes to attain it, or at least to see, hear, or perceive it more deeply. When this mental factor of desire operates in a wholesome way, it has the ability to offer us a foothold into the religious world, as it becomes the basis for the positive mental function of *zeal*. The basic mental function that leads us to take the Buddha-way as a single path from which we do not deviate is desire in a positive mode—wholesome desire.

Devoted interest (adhimukti) is a mental function that acknowledges the object and retains it according to a clearly identifiable way of thinking. This can also function with wholesome, unwholesome, or indeterminate karmic moral quality, but as with the basic nuance of correctness seen in the term *devoted interest,* there is already the anticipation of wholesomeness associated with the term. Indeed, it is explained that it is only in this place that a single, firm, excellent understanding can be established, and where there should be no distraction. In terms of devoted interest, no distraction means that the content of cognition is something that is not easily corrupted.

The mental factor of *mindfulness (smṛti)* preserves the previously cognized object such that is it not forgotten. Because we possess the mental function of being able to powerfully engrave an impression in our minds without forgetting, we can pour our minds into a specifically cognized object. The mental factor that allows us to deeply concentrate feelings on this object without distraction is called *concentration (samādhi)*. This mental factor of *concentration* has the factor of *mindfulness* as its support, and *concentration* in turn serves as the support for the ensuing factor of intelligence.

In Buddhism, concentration is commonly referred to as one of the basic three Buddhist disciplines: moral discipline, concentration, and wisdom. In this case, the term refers specifically to the practice of (seated) meditation, and it is further understood that true wisdom is derived from the mental state produced in this kind of meditative concentration. The object-contingent mental factor of concentration is normally understood in terms of its operation in a wholesome mode, but in terms of its basic potential, it is understood to be capable of operating in all three morally qualitative modes of wholesome, unwholesome, and indeterminate.

Therefore, the form of concentration under discussion here is neither equivalent to *meditative absorption (samāpatti)* nor the concentration listed among the three Buddhist disciplines. Here, concentration refers to a general psychological function of focus, wherein we naturally find ourselves focusing on a single thing in everyday daily experience. This is known technically in Yogācāra as *inherent concentration.*

There are two kinds of concentration understood in Yogācāra Buddhism; the first is this inherent concentration, and the second is *cultivated concentration,* the latter being attained in the course of continuous diligent practice of the Buddhist path. The development of true wisdom is dependent upon the degree to which a practitioner is able to cultivate concentration. However, we cannot but be powerfully encouraged when we consider that there is somehow an intimate connection between the difficult-to-attain cultivated concentration and the general mental function of inherent concentration that is possessed by all of us.

Intelligence (prajñā) is the function of the mind that makes the choice of selecting or rejecting the object of cognition. For example, even though a handbag may look like a genuine Gucci, one's intelligence can discern that it is clearly a fake. Based on this decision, the state of uncertainty as to whether or not it is genuine can be removed. This kind of mental function is labeled intelligence.

The mental factor of intelligence can also work in the modes of wholesome, unwholesome, and indeterminate karmic moral quality. Among these, since intelligence functioning in an unwholesome mode would indicate a mistaken judgment in regard to the object, it is classified under a separate heading as the mental factor of *incorrect view* within the category of afflictions. Mistaken views have incredible power to lead us astray from the Buddha-path. Thus, the role of intelligence as a mental factor is rather prominent as compared with other functions.

While the object-contingent factors are, generally speaking, mental functions that operate within the manifest six consciousnesses of eyes, ears, nose, tongue, body, and mind, this final factor of intelligence is understood as operating not only within the sixth consciousness, but in the subconscious region of the *manas.* As explained above, the *manas* pursues its unbounded obsession with the self without lapse, even at the times when the activity of the sixth consciousness has stopped. In the *manas'* function of deep attachment, it is first necessary to either select or reject the object of attachment. The mental function that offers up the object for attachment by the *manas* is none other than the factor of intelligence from among the object-dependent factors. Therefore, the factor of intelligence as explained in Yogācāra is concomitant not only with the sixth consciousness, but the seventh as well.

UNCATEGORIZED MENTAL FACTORS

The group of uncategorized mental factors includes the four of *drowsiness, regret, discovery,* and *scrutiny.* These four mental functions have features that problematize their categorization into the groups of omnipresent factors, object-contingent, wholesome, afflictions, or secondary afflictions, and so they are collectively grouped under the rubric *uncategorized.*

For instance, these mental activities all operate in the sixth consciousness, and therefore, they can't be categorized in the group of omnipresent factors, which necessarily occur in any situation of the mind-king and mental factors. And, unlike the wholesome and the afflictive factors, their karmic moral quality is indeterminate.

Drowsiness (middha) does not refer to sleep itself, but to the function that occurs at the time we are falling asleep. Drowsiness is that which makes us foggy-minded, as when, in a condition of dull-mindedness or confusion, we cannot accurately cognize things, much less perceive their underlying nature and meaning. It is only when we enter the state of the sound sleep (called extreme drowsiness) that the mental factor of drowsiness is inoperative. This is because at the time of deep sleep, the thinking consciousness has ceased to operate.

Recognition of one's errors (kaukṛtya) is also known by the term *regret.* Such mental attitudes that arise when we reflect on previous actions and experience thoughts of regret are called *recognition of errors.* We may struggle over why we said or did something, and no matter the specifics of related actions and consequences, they cannot result in anything but a state of unease.

This mental factor can function in either wholesome, unwholesome, or morally indeterminate modes. When it functions wholesomely, its basic character is to reflect on our prior wrongdoings, and even though this is not necessarily a bad thing, the mind in this state is not calm. Since a calm response cannot be made, the potential exists to cause problems.

"Reflect, but don't regret."

There are people who engrave this maxim at their places of study. Human beings are surrounded by regret wherever we go in our lives.

As described in the passages on perception and omnipresent factors, *discovery (vitarka)* and *scrutiny (vicāra)* are functions that rely on language to further clarify the cognitive object and deepen investigation of it. These mental factors, based on their function, are said to be aspects of volition and intelligence, but since their function lies within the sixth, thinking consciousness, they cannot be strictly categorized as being either omnipresent or object-contingent.

Chapter Four: Building Up Experience in the Latent Area of the Mind

THE FIRST SUBJECTIVE TRANSFORMER—THE ĀLAYA-VIJÑĀNA

After carrying out a detailed analysis of the mind, the Yogācāras became convinced that it was comprised of eight specific regions constituted by the prior five consciousnesses of eyes, ears, nose, tongue, and body that handle the five senses, along with the thinking consciousness, *manas,* and store consciousness. The Yogācāras posited that these eight kinds of mind-king possessed the ability to subjectively transform everything that surrounds us in the process of three stages, which are known as the three subjective transformations. Among these, the most important is the first subjective transformer, the eighth consciousness, the *ālaya-vijñāna.* In this chapter, we will first take a look at the *ālaya-vijñāna* in its role as the subject that transforms the objects of cognition. *Ālaya* is a Sanskrit word that can be translated as store (or storehouse), and *ālaya-vijñāna* is often rendered into English as the "store consciousness," with the implication that it accumulates and preserves information. What exactly *is* put away in this store consciousness? As a way of getting around to answering this question, we need to first inquire as to which region of consciousness we should regard as being the real center of the mind-kings of the eight consciousnesses. From the perspective of the actual experiences of everyday life, we might well consider the sixth, the thinking consciousness *(mano-vijñāna)* as the center of the mind. We manage our daily lives through the variety of functions governed by the thinking consciousness. However, as we have already mentioned, this thinking consciousness is subject to interruptions—it does not operate continuously.

For example, both fainting and deep sleep bring our thinking consciousness to a halt. While one could argue that the case of fainting is problematic based on the fact that it is such a rare occurrence, deep sleep is a nightly certainty for most people. We understand that even if the thinking mind seems to operate continuously, it is something that is in fact frequently interrupted, existing only as discontiguous fragments. If there were no mental framework to pull these pieces together, we could not exist as integrated beings. The *ālaya-vijñāna* is necessary to serve as the "backup" for intentional, conscious life.

Our actions and behavior are directly related to our interaction with others. After we complete these actions, we can be certain that they will always be evaluated in some way, and we can be sure that the reverberations of these acts will imprint society to one extent or another, whether it be labeled as an "excellent achievement" or a " crime." In both cases we are clearly subjected to, and imprinted with, a social evaluation; yet this social evaluation is only made possible by our actions being seen through the eyes of others.

So what happens when our negative actions are not seen by others? Since no one is watching, the perpetrator of some nasty business assumes that he will never be subject to public evaluation. Afterward, he may hear people say things like "there are really some bad people hanging around, aren't there." Playing dumb, he sticks out his tongue at them behind their backs, and that's the end of it. From the perspective of society, the case is closed. But what ends up happening to such a person on the inside?

Among the three karmic modes of body, speech, and thought, it is only thoughts that are not accessible to others, as they occur inside our mind as mental karma. However, as explained above in the discussion of the mental factor of volition, in Buddhism, even the thoughts that occur within the mind are understood to have a marvelous function.

It is at this point that the Yogācārin asks what, exactly, is the nature of this that we call our actions. The conclusion is that the dispositions of every act end up leaving behind impressions in the *ālaya-vijñāna,* where the after-effects of our activities are retained.

> Although we are careful when we know we are being watched by others, we should not forget that we are also watched by spiritual beings.

These are the words of the Great Japanese Yogācāra master of the Kamakura period, Gedatsu Shōnin (Jōkei; 1155–1213), from his *Gumei hosshin shu (Awakening the Mind From Delusion)*. We are automatically cautious in our actions and speech—the objects of evaluation by others—when we are in the presence of people, but less so when we think we are not being observed, or when the activity is taking place hidden within our minds. Our world of thought that is unknown to others has an amazing proclivity to fall into dissoluteness. However, Gedatsu Shōnin is telling us that this place is perfectly visible to the eyes of the gods and buddhas, meaning that our negative actions never go unwitnessed.

Our world of thought, where we are secretly at ease, is indeed an untidy place. According to the Yogācāras, everything that occurs here turns into a burden which we must carry in a future life. The *ālaya-vijñāna* retains all of our memories up to the present, and all of the dispositions of activities and behavior have been secretly accumulated in the basis of our minds. These are in turn re-manifested and naturally exude from our being. The Yogācāras take this as the most fundamental underlying operation of our minds.

This kind of automatic exuding of the dispositions of our past experiences in the midst of our cognition is called the *first subjective transformation*. The *ālaya-vijñāna* that retains the impressions of all of our past experiences first acts to transform the objects of cognition. We have utterly no conscious control over what we exude. We cannot help but taking that which is first subjectively transformed as a cognitive object, and this subjective transformation is a reflection of our entire past—which is none other than ourselves. When we discuss the store consciousness as the first subjective transformation, we are talking about this fundamental—and somewhat frightening—point.

To the extent that we deepen this kind of contemplation of the ramifications of the store consciousness, we cannot but end up coming to the conclusion that from this moment forward, we must try to orient our lives in some positive direction. Yogācāra Buddhism is asking us to seek out a way of life grounded in such a recognition and awareness. By positing the existence of the *ālaya-vijñāna*, Yogācāra Buddhism strongly suggests that a life of careless behavior won't do.

The Perfuming of Seeds

Consider a famous novelist who is known for revealing his personal thoughts by taking his own life as his subject matter. This doesn't necessarily mean that he has revealed everything there is to know about himself. There is no one who does not have something within himself that he keeps hidden from others. At the same time, we may assume that because our actions were witnessed by others that the case is karmically closed. Indeed, though the case may be closed on the level of society and human interaction, the ramifications of the negative activity do not disappear, and the impressions are long retained.

We then turn to consider by what kind of process, and in what kind of form, our actions and behavior could possibly be retained, and then accumulated, in the mind's innermost depths of the *ālaya-vijñāna*? It is explained in Yogācāra that "manifest activity *perfumes* the seeds in the *ālaya-vijñāna.*" "Manifest activity" can be understood as our concrete activities, and these concrete actions and behaviors end up being "perfumed" into the store consciousness in the form of metaphorical "seeds."

Perfuming means that in the same way that an odor is transferred to and adheres to clothing, one's actions create impressions and dispositions that become planted in the deepest regions of that person's mind where they are retained. These impressions impregnate the store consciousness, and as planted actions, they are called "seeds" as they have the power to give form to the subsequent self.

These seeds, which are secretly impregnated and retained in the *ālaya-vijñāna,* will again generate visible phenomena when the right set of circumstances arises. Since this is exactly the kind of function associated with the physical seeds of plants, they are so named metaphorically. We should not, however, go so far as to construe them as material, substantial seeds.

Seeds are explained as "the power within the eighth consciousness to produce an effect." That is, they represent the causative power to manifest activity as fruit from within the *ālaya-vijñāna.* Seeds represent the momentum of impressions, and also be understood from the perspective of the almost synonymous technical term, *karmic impressions* (Skt. *vāsanā*). Karmic impressions have the connotation of "dispositions caused by perfumation." The notions of seed and perfumation are seminal in Yogācāra Buddhism, and although they may seem to be rather arcane concepts, they are necessary to understanding the operation of karma and consciousness in Yogācāra.

In *The Oriental Ideal (Tōyō no risō)*, Okura Tenjin wrote: "Surely the shadow of the past exists as the promise for the future. No tree can grow larger than the potential contained in its seed." Here the word *seed* is being used in its basic biological sense, rather than as a Yogācāra term, and it can be understood as a general truth. However, truth understood by Yogācāra Buddhism is that what we call "the past" exerts an influence on the formation of the future, and the future is something that cannot be so easily changed. This will be covered in depth in the following section.

I have heard that the former *kyōgen* (a form of traditional Japanese theater) master Miyake Tōkurō, who was famous for the severity of discipline he imposed on himself while practicing, had a saying to the effect that "there is no such thing as luck on the stage," considering "luck" to refer to the case where one performs with good technique by mere coincidence. While some may say that things are "by chance" going well, in truth there is no reason why they should, or continue to do so. A first-rate stage performance depends completely on self-discipline through consistent practice.

That which has not been stored up in the *ālaya-vijñāna* won't suddenly appear at the moment one steps up in front of the footlights. No matter how hard one tries, if the requisite potentiality has not been accumulated in the store consciousness, it cannot be manifested upon demand. The same applies for those of us who do not perform on the stage. And what sort of thing, exactly, is perfumed in our *ālaya-vijñāna*? It is on the answer to this question that we now embark, but replacing the word "stage" with the words "human life," and reinterpreting this saying as "there is no such thing as luck in life."

BEGINNINGLESS PERFUMING

In Yogācāra, it is not the case that our actions, being finished, are simply over with, or that we are no longer responsible for them. After the event,

the perfuming seeds, accumulated in the eighth consciousness as poten-
tialities, are keeping record of everything. If we accept this, then the *ālaya-
vijñāna* becomes understood as being the accumulated totality of life
experiences—nothing other than the present "I." When we think seriously
as to how every one of the actions and behaviors after receiving birth in this
world are impregnated without loss into the mind's innermost depths, and
that this influence continues to extend into our present selves, we cannot
but end up being deeply concerned.

Additionally, in regard to the matter of perfuming, Yogācāra posits
something called *beginningless perfuming*. This means that perfuming has
continued from time immemorial, without beginning, and that the seeds
in the store consciousness are not simply produced beginning with birth
into this present life.

This brings us to consider our attachment to this life—a desire to keep
living. No matter how disappointing or complicated we feel our life has
become, we still want to continue in it for as long as possible. Buddhist
philosophy states that suffering is produced from this attachment to life,
and it is because of this ardent attachment to life that we can continue to
struggle through our daily lives.

Most of us firmly maintain this mental state of ardent attachment right
up to the moment before death. It is quite likely that the thought "I want
to live" that appears at our final moment is the most strongly held feeling
in all of life. Buddhism teaches us that it is precisely because we are so
strongly attached to life down to its very final moment that we cause ourselves to be reborn into the next life. This is called *transmigration*.

This means that the kind of life we are living here and now is precisely
due to the ardent attachment we held for our existence in our former life.
And our former life must be something that was brought about by an
"attachment to life" in the life before that. This being the case, we can
trace our present existence back infinitely into the past. Our store consciousness is not only comprised of all of the actions, dispositions, and
impressions beginning with our birth in this present lifetime, but it is also
perfumed by the seeds of our actions and behavior from all of our lifetimes in the immeasurable past. This is the meaning of "beginningless
perfuming."

Being exposed to this kind of teaching, we naturally become awed at the apparently limitless depth and capacity of this *ālaya-vijñāna,* and concerned about what might be perfumed and contained within us. However, even while wincing at the notion of the vastness of this *ālaya-vijñāna,* we should calmly think, what on earth this "I" is that has been traversing through lifetimes since time immemorial? At such a time, we become newly aware of our ardent attachment to life. With this expression "attachment to life" to replace Yogācāra technical terminology, we may begin to further deepen our mindfulness. In Yogācāra, the cause of reincarnation is assumed to be mental disturbances, which consist more precisely of the mental factors of afflictions and secondary afflictions enumerated in the lists of mental factors in the preceding chapter. It is not explicitly stated in the Yogācāra source texts, but understanding the function of the store consciousness the way it is taught, we can assume that it might, unbeknown to us, be retaining something that reaches all the way back to the very origins of human existence, and life itself. This awareness cannot but give the feeling in each individual that each and every life should be respected as a member of the universe of sentient beings. And, at the same time, each one of us individually needs to be deeply aware of the perspective wherein an attempt is made to live life based on this awareness of respecting every kind of life form.

THREE MEANINGS OF STORE

There are three connotations identified in the earliest Yogācāra texts related to the *ālaya-vijñāna:* (1) the storer (i.e., storing agent); (2) that which is stored; and (3) the appropriated store. Taking these as the fundamental approaches for considering the *ālaya-vijñāna,* we now move to take another look at what we have discussed regarding the *ālaya-vijñāna* and show how it fits into the framework of these three.

(1) The *storer* indicates that this deep mind is something that possesses the basic quality of being able to preserve our experiences in its seeds. It is the "mind that is able to store all seeds." When this is considered from the perspective of the seeds, these are the things that are stored by the *ālaya-vijñāna.* But if the seeds are looked at by themselves, regardless of their

container, the seeds are that which give rise to manifest activity. They are the main causes of the formation of a self. When the *ālaya-vijñāna* is seen from the causal aspect of such a potentiality, it is called the "consciousness containing all seeds."

(2) *That which is stored* connotes the store consciousness as the recipient of perfuming. The seeds that are the impressions and dispositions of our various concrete activities are able to perfume the *ālaya-vijñāna*. If we take this as storer, the *ālaya-vijñāna* that is the recipient of perfuming becomes that which is stored. In this way, that which is stored becomes the recipient of perfuming. But if this is seen from the perspective of actions and behavior, the *ālaya-vijñāna* that undergoes the perfuming also exists as the result of these activities.

The eighth consciousness seen from this aspect of effect is called the *ripening consciousness* (Skt. *vipāka-vijñāna*). The *ālaya-vijñāna* continues without break from the past to the future, and serves as a backup for the intermittently functioning thinking consciousness. In Yogācāra Buddhism, this eighth consciousness that serves as the basis for human existence is originally of neither wholesome nor unwholesome karmic moral quality, and thus it is said to be of indeterminate (or neutral) karmic moral character.

If this very fundamental source of our existence were intrinsically bad, we would end up cycling again and again through a world of suffering, unable to obtain a foothold to Buddha's world throughout all eternity. On the other hand, if our fundamental basis was intrinsically good, and all people's minds were connected to the buddha-mind, it would be difficult to reconcile this with our everyday experiences in society.

It is also not the case that the variety of our daily activities and behaviors clearly tend in one direction or the other. This is made clear by merely looking at the fifty-one mental factors considered above in chapter 3. Even while we lust after something, we may at the same time reflect strongly on our lust. While diligently devoting ourselves to the Buddha-path, we may inadvertently give rise to anger. Our basic nature is not disposed toward either goodness or evil, but is of indeterminate moral karmic quality.

We are, without doubt, planting the seeds of goodness in the store consciousness with our wholesome activities, and impregnating it with bad impression-potential with our unwholesome activities. This is possible precisely because the eighth consciousness has no fundamental predisposition toward good or evil—it is of indeterminate karmic moral quality. Depending on the seeds of good or evil that have already been planted, various real and concrete good and evil activities occur. Nevertheless, the eighth consciousness does not incline toward good or evil. Individual actions taken by themselves, along with the perfuming from their impressions, can be wholesome, unwholesome, or indeterminate in karmic moral quality, but if the *ālaya-vijñāna* as the result of activities is viewed as a whole, it is neither good nor evil.

Just as wholesome causes bring wholesome effect and unwholesome causes bring unwholesome effects, cause and effect are understood to be imbued with the same karmic moral quality (in Yogācāra, this condition is denoted with the technical term *continuity of sameness,* or *natural outcome;* Skt. *nisyanda*). But in the *ālaya-vijñāna*-as-effect, whether or not it is produced by a good or bad seed, the end result of the action is always understood to be of indeterminate or neutral moral quality. This kind of cause-effect relationship is called ripening, and because the *ālaya-vijñāna* as the aspect of effect is seen in this way, it is called the *ripening consciousness.* In other words, in its ripened state it has a different karmic moral quality than its causes. When one thing produces another, the next thing that is produced, while having a direct and close relation to its cause, must also be something different from its cause. Common metaphors include that of the ripening of a fruit, or a baked loaf of bread, which are both quite different in character from their causal stages, and have exhausted their potential for further development.

This aspect of the *ālaya-vijñāna* of being of intrinsically indeterminate moral quality is vitally important from a religious perspective. Although we humans are greatly influenced by our own past, we are at the same time endowed with the potential of creating an entirely different future, starting right here and now, no matter how deeply our past is filled with evil karma. But on the other hand, even if our days were filled with efforts toward cultivating buddhahood, we can never assume that we have safely achieved a level of perfection.

(3) *Appropriated store* refers to the attachment to self-love. We have the feeling that we are spending every day living in a conscious manner. However,

as we have already seen, the operations of the thinking consciousness and prior five consciousnesses are intermittent and are broadly supported by the basis of human existence, the *ālaya-vijñāna*. In Yogācāra Buddhism, it is thought that the only reason we are able to live such a unified existence is because of the store consciousness.

The *ālaya-vijñāna* is a mental region which has arrived to the present in a continuous unbroken stream while receiving uninterrupted beginningless perfuming from the past. And it will continue unbroken into the future. The great Indian master Vasubandhu, who is accorded the bulk of the credit for the foundation of Yogācāra Buddhism, described the *ālaya-vijñāna* in his *Triṃśikā ("Thirty Verses on Consciousness-only")* as "constantly coming forth, like a raging current." Our deep *ālaya-vijñāna* is like a great river, which, while roiling in turbulence from the eternal upstream, rolls without stopping on its way downstream. This store consciousness has always been in a state of continuous alteration.

However, while it is not something immutable, it has the character of being *changeless but changing.* The seventh consciousness, the *manas,* functions in a way of trying to see the unchanging aspect of the store consciousness as an immutable essence. The *manas* takes this ostensive immutable essence as its object and adheres firmly to it, believing it to be a self. This kind of misconstrual and reification of the *ālaya-vijñāna* on the part of the *manas* constitutes the third connotation of store: *appropriated store.*

While in Yogācāra Buddhism the *ālaya-vijñāna* is interpreted with these three connotations of storer, that which is stored, and appropriated store, it is the meaning of appropriated store that tends to be paid the greatest attention. The aspect of existence that is reified by the *manas* is the characteristic of the *ālaya-vijñāna* itself. The Yogācāras argue that the very core of suffering is to be found in the place where the *manas,* the mind of attachment to the ego—engages itself in the activity of attachment, taking the *ālaya-vijñāna* as its object. Thus we can say that the meaning of the appropriated store defines the relation between the eighth, *ālaya-vijñāna,* and the seventh, *manas,* consciousnesses.

Continuity of Sameness

So the relation of the *manas* to the *ālaya-vijñāna* is that the *manas,* the mind of ego-attachment, taking the deep store consciousness as its object, misconstrues it to be the reified essence of the self, and strongly clings to it, and within this relationship, Yogācāra Buddhism sees the causes of all human problems. Therefore, among the three connotations—storer, the stored, and appropriated store—the connotation of appropriated store is the most fundamental from a religious perspective.

The store consciousness that undergoes beginningless perfuming is taken as the object of attachment of the *manas* because of the existence of a mental region—a psychological basis—that appears as changing-but-unchanging, and functions to maintain something that resembles a self-identity. This special characteristic of the *ālaya-vijñāna* is called *continuity of type* or *continuity of identity.* Continuing in a single type means that an unchanging character continues without interruption.

Within the store consciousness there exists a characteristic of continuity in sameness that has continued changelessly and without interruption from the distant past. And the store consciousness, with its indeterminate karmic moral character, is that which takes our daily behaviors and activities that are riddled with interruptions, binds them together, accumulates them, and unifies them.

Dealing with Impermanence and No-Self

The three most fundamental principles that are said to specially identify the Buddhist teachings are (1) impermanence of all phenomena; (2) the selflessness of all phenomena; and (3) the quiescence of nirvāṇa. These are three distinctive characteristics that mark a given set of teachings as being authentically Buddhist, and any teaching not based on these three can be said to be non-Buddhist. Within ourselves and the natural world, all things arise, cease, and change. That such arising and cessation occurs every single instant is the meaning of the impermanence of all phenomena. This is the most fundamental concept in Buddhism.

At first glance, we may be inclined to regard this fact as being patently obvious. No doubt we all understand that all things are constantly changing. Nonetheless, we may not be comfortable with things that are always in a state of flux, as it makes us ill at ease. We struggle to take things that are in flux and continually force them into our framework, reifying and trying to grasp them, while at the same time reifying the understanding gained through this process. Isn't this the way we are functioning every day?

Without a doubt, we are enriching our lives as we accumulate new experiences daily. However, as we age we become increasingly aware of the falloff in our ability to recover from physical fatigue. If at this point we reflect back on our twenties and thirties, we become newly aware of the subtle changes in our physical strength. And we recall that people tried to warn us, but we were too young and proud to take heed. Yet even while we come to understand that our bodies and minds are always changing, we also retain a distinct sense of being thoroughly penetrated by the changing-yet-unchanging.

Some philosophical schools of ancient India were convinced that this changing-but-unchanging aspect existed in people as an immutable essence, and they called it *ātman* ("I," self, soul). This *ātman* was understood to be the subject of transmigration, something immortal, running through the past and future repeatedly through our life and death. But if all things are transient, how can we acknowledge the existence of this kind of invariable, immortal *ātman*? This kind of substantial self was clearly denied by the Buddha, and this idea is the meaning of selflessness of all phenomena.

Even though we understand intellectually that our ego can't be an immutable essence, we still seek such an essence in ourselves and grasp to it, and as a result bind ourselves. The Buddha Śākyamuni called on us to turn against this unfortunate urge, and try to bravely manage our lives based on the realities of impermanence and no-self. He taught that a life lived in accordance with these kinds of realities leads us to a state that is spontaneously and genuinely free of restrictions, and completely pure. This is the quiescence of nirvāṇa, a state of calm manifested in body and mind, within which one harmonizes with reality.

There is a problem here, though, since in addition to the three seals of the dharma, Buddhism includes the notion of reincarnation as one of its basic tenets. Given the doctrine of no-self, what should we understand to be the subject that repeatedly undergoes this birth and death? In ancient India, it was thought that we undergo repeated reincarnation with a substantial, immortal self as subject. But because the Buddha categorically denied such a thing as an eternal *ātman,* Buddhism had to locate a subject of transmigration without undermining the theory of no-self. After the Buddha's death, various theories about this were tendered by a number of Buddhist groups. The most well thought-out resolution of this problem is that of the *ālaya-vijñāna,* as posited by the Yogācāras. As an answer to the nonexistence of an enduring essence, they saw a latent mind that continues with the same morally indeterminate karmic quality, storing and accumulating the impressions of past experiences as seeds of potentiality for the production of effects. This, they posited as the subject of reincarnation.

Summary: If Things Can't Be So Simply Washed Away, Then What?

In the thinking consciousness *(mano-vijñāna),* the experiences of our daily lives are quickly forgotten. We may read a novel with great passion, but undoubtedly after the passage of several years, it will be difficult to recall portions of its plot. However, even if it is completely forgotten on the side of the thinking consciousness, it is properly stored in the subconscious region.

We can say that in having this kind of store consciousness that preserves our entire past, our present selves exist atop that same storehouse, which serves as our foundation. In this sense, our past actions and experiences cannot be so easily washed away. But within the range of our memory we may tend to try to wash away the recollection of inconvenient events, to act as if they never existed.

The notion of "washing away" is well understood among the Japanese people in particular. Perhaps there may even be some sense in which consciously dealing with the past is related to a particular cultural ethos. Whether or not this is true, if light is shed on the matter from a Yogācāra perspective, the mere mutual agreement to forget about an incident only amounts to being the most superficial manner of handling a past problem. Our present existence is constituted by the things we have done in the past, no matter how ugly they may be. The problem is what, exactly, we are perfuming into our *ālaya-vijñāna.*

In the world of Buddhism, cultivation of a particular aspect of our spirit and body is often carried out in a traditional format within a set period of time, and we call this "practice. " But when we exert ourselves in the effort of valuing our daily life as it is, trying not to be sloppy in the three karmic activities of body, speech, and thought, this is not simply called "practice"; rather, it is labeled with the Buddhist technical term *applied practice* (Skt. *prayoga*). This means that, when, on the other hand, practice is not "applied," we are doubtlessly carrying out our daily life in a sloppy way.

Applied practice refers to this kind of maintenance of continual mindfulness. For instance, in the *Avalokiteśvara Sūtra*[3] the term *constant mindfulness* appears often, advising one to be continuously mindful of the Bodhisattva Avalokiteśvara. As a result, the Bodhisattva Avalokiteśvara is gradually impressed strongly into the mind's innermost depths, and the mindfulness of Avalokiteśvara is accumulated in the *ālaya-vijñāna.* We develop a focused spiritual power, which becomes a support and foundation for future practices.

The past cannot be altered, or brushed off by excuses. We are nothing but a vast, unerring receptacle of our past. And regardless of our past experiences, it is our past in its totality that is the basis of our being. Yet we can, taking this totality as our basis, from this moment forward align ourselves with the Buddha's teaching with a view toward tomorrow. This is the beginning of a life based on the wisdom of Yogācāra.

The possibility for this lies in none other than the fact that the *ālaya-vijñāna* is an ever-ripening consciousness. Although we are standing on an inescapable past, we are existing here and now, in a present state of neither good nor evil—indeterminacy. The Buddha warned us how ill-will can instantly incinerate the forest of merit built with great effort, and thus we should strive to focus and rise above our past indiscretions. In the wonderful words of the *Sūtra of the Deathbed Injunction:*[4] "The one who practices forbearance is a great man possessed of power." However, even if one is a great man possessed of power, if he gives rise to anger even once, he is no better than an ordinary person.

The fact that we rest upon this firm foundation of the past, and simultaneously have the ability to anticipate a bright future, is our way of being, all contained with in the deeply abiding *ālaya-vijñāna*.

Chapter Five: The Production of Things

THE CONSCIOUSNESS CONTAINING ALL SEEDS

If the only function of the *ālaya-vijñāna* were to secretly preserve and accumulate all the impressions of all the activities in our entire past experiences without the slightest bit of loss, it would not act as a source of pain or irritation for us. The problem lies in the fact that the dispositions of past experiences go on to become the major causal factors in the formation of the subsequent "I."

The term "seeds" refers to nothing other than the potential energy, under the right conditions, to produce subsequent manifest activities related to those that preceded. Seeds can be characterized as "the potential within the eighth consciousness to produce an effect." Yesterday's conduct and today's activity produce what will end up being the self of tomorrow, and the function and power that brings about such a result is called "seeds."

The *ālaya-vijñāna* is called "consciousness containing all seeds" *(sarva-bījaka-vijñāna),* signifying that the impression-dispositions of the past actions and behavior saved in the eighth consciousness end up being the primary causes for the production of *dharmas* of the future. The term *all dharmas* (Skt. *sarva-dharma*) is very common in Buddhist discourse, and so we should provide a very basic explanation of its connotations. Although the range of meanings of *dharma* is extremely broad, I would like to focus here on the two most important meanings that relate to our present discussion.

The first usage is like that seen in the case of the term *buddha-dharma.* The teachings given by the Buddha are called the buddha-dharma, which is commonly expressed simply as *dharma.* When we see such expressions as "seek the dharma" or "for the purpose of the dharma," this is a reference to dharma as *teaching*.

The second major connotation of the term *dharma*, which is being invoked in the expression *all dharmas*, is the sense of *existence* or *thing*. The term *all dharmas* has the meaning of *all things* or *all phenomena*, referring to all existing things and phenomena. As you may recall, above we introduced the name of the East Asian transmission of the Yogācāra school as the "Dharma-Characteristics" School (in Chinese, Faxiang School, in Japanese, Hossō School), and the usage of dharma there also implies this meaning of *all existences* and *everything*. The Dharma-Characteristics School tended to take a special interest in ascertaining and explaining the true character of these dharmas.

Further, the *production of all dharmas* refers to the appearance of all phenomena in our daily lives, and included within this is the formation of our own selves. The causal power for the occurrence of such dharmas is the seeds that are stored in the *ālaya-vijñāna*. Within the function of these seeds, according to the presence of the right conditions, phenomena are manifested before our eyes. Our own behavior also becomes a manifest actuality, and is no longer mere potentiality.

SEEDS AND MANIFEST ACTIVITY

The term *manifest activity perfuming seeds* refers to seeds that represent the momentum of the impressions of manifest activity that is impregnated into the *ālaya-vijñāna*—those same manifest activities originally produced by seeds. This process of seeds giving rise to manifest phenomena is called *seeds generating manifest activity*.

In Yogācāra Buddhism, these two functions are never conceived of as operating as two distinct processes, but are always understood to be linked as one—seeds generating manifest activity / manifest activity perfuming seeds. The continuous cycle operates in such a way that the seeds that are the disposition-impressions of past experiences give rise to present actualities and activities, and the impressions of those activities are again stored in the *ālaya-vijñāna*.

To express this, there is the concept of "three successive processes simultaneously bringing about cause and effect." These three processes are: (1) the creation of seeds from manifest activity; (2) the production of manifest activity from seeds, and (3) the perfuming of those seeds already contained in the *ālaya-vijñāna* by manifest activities. The fact that these three phenomena, while acting as mutual causes and effects, continuously operate one after the other, and that furthermore all of this happens simultaneously, is called *three successive processes bringing about cause and effect simultaneously.*

This is said to happen instantaneously, and according to Yogācāra, in less than an instant the manifest activities produced from the seeds of the reverberations of past activities are again stored into the *ālaya-vijñāna* as their seeds and dispositions. Since this phenomenon has continued without interruption since the immeasurably distant past, it is identical to the beginningless perfuming mentioned previously. The occurrence that we call three successive processes bringing about cause and effect simultaneously gives us a rich sense of a flawlessly functioning system that accepts no excuses.

It is easy for us to dismiss our habitual conduct as just something that everyone else does, and thus not worthy of special reflection. Certainly, our everyday selves are nothing other than part of our everyday scenery, and self-reflection is a uncomfortable and difficult mode to remain in. Nonetheless, being based on three successive phenomena bringing about cause and effect simultaneously and beginningless perfuming, what we will come to be in the future is deeply rooted in the everyday behavior we have been engaged in up to now. And while taking a thorough look at ourselves is of vital importance in any circumstance, it is nothing less than indispensable in the religious world. It is only through this process that a firm foundation may be built for the attainment of liberation. Real self-reflection can only happen in the context of everyday, normal activity.

Although I have no formal training in the martial arts, the traditional art of *kyūdō* (traditional Japanese archery) has always moved me. *Kyūdō* requires that an incredible level of mindfulness be exercised up to the moment of the release of the arrow, a level of mindfulness impossible for the impatient. And once the arrow is released, excuses are meaningless. One concentrates the mind and body fully on a single point: the distant target.

In *kyūdō,* there is an incredible level of fine-tuning involved in focusing body and mind, to the extent that one feels a moment of unity between one's mind, body, and the target. Even if the arrow that is boldly released after this fine-tuning does not hit the target, one still feels a sense of calm, a feeling that stems from the fact that one still retains the mental and physical harmonization with the target. Using this analogy, we can clearly perceive the meaning of the mechanism of the seeds and manifest activities operating through the three successive dharmas. By handling the affairs of our daily life with the same attitude, we are removing the necessity for excuses in not hitting the target in archery.

Compared to other religious and philosophical systems, Buddhism pays a considerably greater amount of attention to the matter of the inseparability of cause and effect. It is reiterated that all dharmas do not occur other than their basis in cause and effect, making it impossible to imagine that things have evolved by some sort of accident. This is one of the most fundamental aspects of the Buddhist way of thinking. Tradition says that the Buddha, when delivering his first sermon at the Deer Park in Benares, instructed his students with the *Four Noble Truths* and *Noble Eightfold Path,* with the concepts of cause and effect seminal to this teaching. The Four Noble Truths are: the (1) truth of suffering, (2) truth of arising, (3) truth of cessation, and (4) truth of the path.

(1) The truth of suffering clarifies the most fundamental view of Buddhism—that human life is fundamentally unsatisfactory. But can we all not attest that there exists much great joy within our daily living? Our happiness often acts as our daily target, the only thing getting us through days otherwise filled with anger and frustration. But we have come to understand that this enjoyment is transitory. It is too often our experience that when we continue to do something to excess because of the pleasure it brings, that feeling of enjoyment will eventually turn into pain. This is because our existence is based on suffering, even the pleasurable parts.

The Buddha taught that there are eight kinds of suffering. In addition to the four basic types of birth, aging, sickness, and death, we also suffer from separation from pleasurable things (or the people we like); association with undesirable things (or the people we dislike); not getting what we desire; and we suffer from existing within the unstable flux of the five aggregates. This last kind of suffering is a bit of catch-all for various kinds of suffering, but mainly refers to the suffering we experience in relation to our inability to determine, locate, and account for who we really are, given the fact that we are composed of a wide range of unstable physical and mental factors that are roughly categorized into five groups, known as the "five aggregates." For example, we have the strong desire to maintain eternal youth, despite gradual weakening and aging, and this conflict between our desire and the actuality cannot but bring about discomfort.

(2) The truth of arising identifies mental disturbances (afflictions) or actions and behaviors (karma) as the causes of human suffering. Since suffering occurs because of mental disturbances and karma, it is called *suffering from afflicted activity*.

(3) The third truth, that of cessation, tells us that if we sever the mental disturbances and karma that are the causes of suffering, we can obtain nirvana (peace of mind). The truth of cessation is identified as the true purpose of human existence.

(4) Finally, the truth of the path indicates the method and process by which tranquillity is attained. This path is presented as a list of eight items to be practiced in daily life: right view, right thought, right speech, right action, right livelihood, right effort, right mindfulness, and right concentration.

Within these four truths, we can see the significance of cause-and-effect within Buddhist philosophy. In the first two truths, there is (1) the suffering of human existence (effect) and (2) the mental disturbances and karma that bring it about (cause). In the second two truths, (3) the liberation that is the true goal of human life (effect) is brought about by (4) the daily practice of the eightfold path (cause). The former pair represents an analysis of the actual present human condition, while the latter pair is related to the attainment of liberation. These are known respectively as *tainted cause-and-effect* and *untainted cause-and-effect*.[5] Buddhist philosophy strives to first try to fully comprehend the cause and effect relationships that bring about the actual human condition before progressing further down the path.

The classical Buddhist scholastic text *Abhidharmakośa-bhāsya* elaborates upon the topic of cause and effect as the theory of *six causes, four conditions,* and *five kinds of effects*. In that text, a detailed and precise examination was carried out regarding the causes and conditions involved in the production of all dharmas. Within these causes and conditions, four general categories were posited, which include: (1) direct causes; (2) causation through similar and immediately antecedent conditions; (3) objective referent as cause/condition; (4) contingent factors as causes and conditions.

Yogācāra Buddhism took this set of four and further elaborated them in this way: (1) A *direct cause* is an immediate cause that produces all the phenomena we experience in our everyday lives. The seeds stored in the *ālaya-vijñāna* function to produce manifest activities. From this perspective, the causes are the seeds. Then, the manifest activities that were produced by the seeds immediately perfume the impression-momentum seeds in the *ālaya-vijñāna* and in this way those manifest activities are the direct causes of those seeds. Thus there are two kinds of direct causes: seeds as direct cause, and manifest activity as direct cause. With these two as condition, all dharmas are produced, an effect that we call *seeds producing manifest activity, manifest activity perfuming seeds.*

(2) *Causation through similar and immediately antecedent conditions* refers to a situation wherein a certain type of mental function (mind-king or mental factor) occurs continuously, with the antecedent mind-king/mental factor becoming the condition for the succeeding mind-king/mental factor. There is no interruption between past and present, leading to what is called a similar and immediately antecedent condition.

(3) The *objective referent as cause* refers to the causative power of the objects of cognition. If an object of cognition is not present as a condition, cognitive function cannot occur, since the projected image (objective aspect) that is manifested in the mind fails to appear. Raw sensate appearances (the things of the external world) both give rise to objective aspects and are indirect cognitive objects, and as such they are included in the category of objective referent as cause.

(4) *Contingent factors as causes and conditions* refers to the ancillary causes and conditions that function in the production of all dharmas, lying beyond the scope of the three causes and conditions introduced above. While the primary requirement in the production of effects is the direct cause, cooperative factors are also necessary—there has to be a

friendly, supportive environment in order for things to occur—or at least an environment that does not *prevent* the occurrence of something. These are the contingent causes. The former case has an active connotation which is called *supporting contingent factors,* and since the latter case is merely a lack of obstruction, it is called *non-obstructing contingent factors.*

The dharmas (in this case, often rendered into English as *elements* or *factors*) are divided into two broad categories: mind dharmas (mental factors), and form dharmas (material factors). Mind dharmas occur based on all four kinds of causes and conditions, while form dharmas are produced by two kinds of causes and conditions (direct causes and contingent factors). Material things are established based on seeds in the store consciousness.

By now we can see how Yogācāra Buddhism explains the occurrence of things mainly through the concepts of *seeds* and *manifest activity.* Since use of the term *all dharmas* has a tendency to depersonalize this process, we should reiterate that point that what is being referred to is nothing other than the content of our daily activities. And the fact that these daily activities occur based on nothing other than the seeds amassed in our *ālaya-vijñāna* means that the responsibility for what occurs in our life is entirely our own. When we are handling things well, we tend to see the causes for success as coming from within ourselves. But when things are not going well, we tend to shift the responsibility and blame to someone else, or to some external factor. The fact that such shenanigans are utterly in vain is due to the fact of the seeds and the manifest activity being direct causes.

In the meaning of "non-obstructing" we can see the breadth of the Buddhist vision in its taking into account ancillary conditions in the production and establishment of each thing. Even the little mundane features of our lives that are passed by and ignored contribute to the constitution of the present "I" at that moment. This realization makes it more difficult to ignore the consequences of all of our daily interactions. And when thinking about supporting causes beyond those of immediate motivation, we can think of ourselves as profoundly situated on top of a vast and fertile ground of production.

Although the manifest activities produced from the seeds plant new impressions back into the *ālaya-vijñāna* as seeds simultaneously with their own production, it is not necessarily the case that seeds perfumed to the *ālaya-vijñāna* immediately re-generate new effects. There are, in fact, an overwhelming number of circumstances in which manifest activity cannot be directly attained. This means that the necessary conditions must be anticipated and prepared in order for any event to occur.

Here a problem arises: if the necessary conditions are absent, what happens to those seeds? Eishun (1518–1596) of Kōfukuji Temple in the Muromachi period had this to say:

> Whatever the experience may be, it cannot avoid being retained by the reliable and incorruptible seeds.

In a diary entry from the twenty-ninth day of the twelfth lunar month in the sixteenth year of Tenshō (1588), he wrote:

> This means simply that seeds do not decompose.

In this way, the impressions and dispositions that are retained in the depths of our minds do not disappear simply because there is no suitable environment for their manifestation. The seeds in the *ālaya-vijñāna* that are the causes for the production for the fruit as manifest activity are, in a latent condition, repeatedly produced and extinguished from moment to moment, while simultaneously transmitting and continuing their character, awaiting the proper environment for their manifestation.

This process is called *seeds generating seeds.* These two kinds of seeds—those that produce and those that are produced—exist in causal relation to each other. The preceding seeds (cause) produce the subsequent seeds (effect). Because cause and effect are temporal, it is not a simultaneous relationship as in *seeds generating manifest activity and manifest activity perfuming seeds,* and so it is called *diachronic cause and effect.*

The process of seeds bringing about the continuity in type while repeatedly being extinguished and reproduced is precisely what is meant by *seeds generating seeds.* Earlier we described the *ālaya-vijñāna's* aspect of preserving the continuity of a single type of quality, but this was only one characterization of the aspect of the *ālaya-vijñāna* as essence. From the aspect of its function, it is characterized as *seeds generating seeds.* Thus, the relationship between the *ālaya-vijñāna* and the seeds can be described as that of the relation between essence and function—aside from seeds, there is nothing in the *ālaya-vijñāna* that we can really speak of.

This further clarifies the point that since seeds generate further seeds in this way, it would be foolish to imagine that the seeds planted by our actions, behavior, and past experiences will naturally fade away over time. The past is something from which we may not escape. We are, no matter what, nothing other than the receptacle of our own past. By keeping keen awareness of the mental processes of *seeds generating manifest activity, manifest activity perfuming seeds* and *seeds generating seeds,* we can begin to behave accordingly and start to follow the Yogācāra way of life. This entails paying continual attention to the fact that our activities proceed through the three karmic processes of bodily activity, speech, and thought, and that every thought passing through our mind has its implications for the future.

INNATE SEEDS AND NEWLY PERFUMED SEEDS

The manifest activities produced from seeds have a single clear result, and manifest activities that appear as effects on the surface have a clearly discernible moral quality to their content. Our daily life is composed by the proliferation of such manifest activities, which develop variously.

Seeds are a way of describing the causal power that will produce results. Since these seeds exist in a latent, unmanifest condition, and are said to be the result *beginningless perfuming,* we have no way to discern their contents. Being unknowable, they defy any sort of observation or evaluation. Since they are unknowable, that means that there is virtually nothing that we can consciously do about them—despite the primacy of their role as the causes of the production of all experienced phenomena.

This means that if I want to try to live from tomorrow according to a Buddhist lifestyle, I have no other recourse but to start not with the unknowable seeds, but the *manifest activities* that are their tangible effects. One voluntarily reflects on one's own manifest activities while receiving the evaluation of others, and based on that creates new behavior. This gradual progression provides us with the opportunity for self-examination within manifest activity.

However manifest activity is something that is characterized by interruptions, which means that no matter how carefully we observe our manifest activity, we cannot come near to knowing the true manner of our own existence by this alone. The seeds both give the main form to our life and serve as its "backup." The main "interactive" processes are those of *seeds generating manifest activity* and *manifest activity perfuming seeds*. But in terms of the problem of bringing about changes in our being, we need to pay special attention to the process that preserves the continuity of sameness in kind, which is the mechanism of *seeds generating seeds*. When we discuss a person's character or basic personality, we must learn to go beyond the range of externally expressed manifest activity and proceed to take into account the latent, unmanifest seeds. Otherwise, we can never gain a sense of the person in his or her entirety.

Manifest activities are nothing more than the behavior constituted by individual actions. That which unites a person's separate manifest actions into an integrated whole is the extent to which they "seem like him" or reflect his individual potential. If we miss this aspect, then even if we have gained a certain sense of the person by accurately observing his separately apparent actions, and even if this sense may seem to tally with what that person really is in his integrated totality, in the final analysis, it has to be different. In order to approach the true aspect of a human being, great consideration needs to be given to the seeds, or the *ālaya-vijñāna,* even though we have no conscious access to them.

The factors that form the totality of someone's character, or personality, are usually distinguished—in all ages and all cultures—into those that are inherent and those that are acquired. Thus, when discussing a person's personality, we often refer to her or his "nature." By *inherent* we mean something that is inborn and not readily changeable—which lacks room for the effects of education and training. As distinguished from the inherent, the *acquired* is that which is assimilated into the person after birth, such as influences stemming from familial environments or social norms that are naturally ingrained; or that which one gains based on one's own application of effort. Psychological theories regarding the formation of personality have shown a tendency to incline in one of these two directions (i.e. the timeless debate regarding *nature* vs. *nurture*). Nowadays, it seems to be generally understood that personality formation happens through the course of a dynamic relationship of various mutual influences between the innate and the acquired.

Yogācāra presents a classification in seed theory that separates types of seeds in a way that resembles this nature vs. nurture paradigm. This is the division between what are known as *innate seeds* and *newly perfumed seeds.* The concept of *innate seeds* (or *originally existent* seeds) expresses the potentiality for the production of all dharmas naturally included since the beginningless past in the *ālaya-vijñāna*. Since the term *inherent* indicates original peculiarity, innate seeds can be seen as being analogous to the notion of an inherent tendency. However, since they are possessed "originally, from the beginningless past," it is important to realize that this is something with significantly more complex connotations than those of simply *inborn* or *innate,* as is understood in present-day psychological discourse.

Newly perfumed seeds are seeds that were not originally present in our bodies and minds at birth. These are the impression-dispositions that are newly impregnated from various manifest activities. From the perspective of the classification of personality-forming factors into "acquired" and "inherent," it is possible to think of these newly perfumed seeds in terms of those that are acquired. Since their perfuming is seen to be something that has continued from the beginningless past, the newly perfumed seeds can be understood as included in the category that we normally consider as *inherent.*

It is often said by those comparing modern psychology with Yogācāra that innate seeds are like inborn nature, while newly perfumed seeds are akin to acquired conditioning. In Yogācāra, however, the distinction between innate and acquired is not simply a matter of whether or not the qualities are "inborn," but a question of whether they are naturally accumulated in the basis of our existence from the eternal past. It is thought that these inherent qualities and the non-inherent newly perfumed qualities produce all dharmas based on their mutual relationships, bringing forth the actuality of our life. While this kind of distinction may be hypothetically made, actually identifying distinct seeds as differing along these lines is somewhat problematic. We may say, in a general sense, that innate seeds are originally equipped in the "I," and newly perfumed seeds are newly planted in the *ālaya-vijñāna* based on the activities our daily life, but it is in fact impossible to make a concrete distinction between those that are inherent and those that are newly perfumed. Only the buddhas have the ability to discern this sort of thing.

Instead of getting tangled up in this matter, it is more worthwhile to earnestly contemplate how our present daily actions and behavior are planting newly perfumed seeds in the *ālaya-vijñāna*. So here, again, we return our attention to manifest activity. It is also not helpful to merely (and perhaps, fatalistically) regard our manifest appearance and behavior as the generated effects of seeds; rather, it is more important to see our manifest behavior as the causes for the perfuming of seeds which bring influence on all of our subsequent actions and behavior, as well as our entire future destiny.

The character of such a moment in the linking between manifest activity and (newly perfumed) seeds is well expressed in the following short passage from the *Tale of the Vegetable Roots* (1602) by Hong Zicheng of the Ming period. It contemplates the weaknesses of human beings who retrogress after gradually reaching to a certain kind of level.

> While on the path of desire, you should not be so quick to stick
> your finger in the pot to get a taste. Once you stick your finger in,
> you fall down a thousand fathoms. While on the path of principle,
> you should be on guard not to hesitate and retreat. Retreating once,
> you fall back the distance of a thousand mountains.

The interpretation of this sentence by Usaburo Imai, included in his translation of the text, is as follows:

> Don't temporarily put out your hand thinking to grab an easy
> opportunity to satisfy yourself. Trying to snatch one time, you end
> up falling into the depths of ten thousand fathoms (in other words,
> once you get a taste and remember that taste, you'll end up being
> drowned in it). (On the contrary), when it comes to the path of
> principle, even if you find the difficulty bothersome, don't shrink
> back for a moment. If you shrink back just once, you'll end up being

separated by a thousand mountains' distance which can never be recovered (because once you regard the task as bothersome, it will only become more and more bothersome).[6]

Who can disagree?

We all have the tendency, whatever the situation, to opt for the easiest way out. By repeatedly continuing in this activity we become habituated. At length, coming to an awareness of this, we realize that it shouldn't be, and the mental factor of regret (Skt. *kaukṛtya*) begins to take hold. Is this not our most authentic mode of being? Yet still, even though we are aware that we shouldn't do such-and-such a thing, we gradually slide back into an easy direction. While one can always make the excuse that we are "only human," the awareness brought about from the Yogācāra perspective should help to prevent us from becoming fully immersed in pleasure and ease.

Six Connotations of Seeds

As we have now come to realize, the Yogācāra view is that the two processes of seeds and manifest activity, while serving as mutual cause and effect, produce all appearances, events, and actions. Our daily lives revolve through the chain of links of *seeds generating manifest activity* and *manifest activity perfuming seeds*. In considering the fact that each one of our activities in daily life perfumes its impression into the mind's innermost depths, and these are accumulated as a potential energy for the subsequent production of all dharmas, we shouldn't be able to engage so lightly in careless activity.

On the other hand, this should not be taken as an excuse for not taking action. We can gain greater awareness of the state of mind that bends the bow toward the distantly-placed target. In the final analysis, what is most important is to simply have a target. In his research on the *Vimalakīrti-sūtra,* Dr. Hashimoto Hōkei has said, "the target is that which serves to gather all the power that a person has." Since this is an expression of his own experience in pulling the bow, it is not mere word play. He also said, "Every person should always have a destination."[7]

It doesn't matter whether we call it a target or a destination. In life, if one has a goal, and one fixes one's gaze on it from afar, one will, as a human being, naturally strive for it.

THE SIX CONNOTATIONS

The seeds that represent the *potential within the eight consciousnesses to produce an effect* are understood as operating governed by six different conditions, which are (1) momentariness; (2) simultaneity with their manifestations; (3) functioning in tandem with the appropriate consciousness; (4) having the same karmic quality as their manifestations; (5) production of their manifestations only after the necessary associated causes are present; (6) each seed produces its own peculiar manifestation and no other. These are known as the *six conditions of seeds.* We need to take a moment here and briefly discuss the connotations of each of these distinctive properties in terms of the explanation of seeds given above, especially in terms of the relationship between seeds and manifest activity.

(1) *Momentariness* means that seeds, representing the potentiality for the production of all things, arise, cease, and change without interruption. If it were the case that seeds were something eternal and unchanging, causation would be rendered impossible. The fact that seeds cannot be something eternal and unchanging, but must arise, cease, and change from moment to moment, is the meaning of momentariness.

Next we move to the condition of simultaneous cause and effect as an aspect of the causes and effects in the production of all phenomena, which is the relationship between seeds and manifest activity. This is the meaning of (2) *simultaneity of seeds with their manifestations.* This means that seeds, as the causes for the production of all dharmas, simultaneously contain their effect *qua* manifest activity. This idea was already touched upon in some detail from the perspective of the *three successive phenomena bringing about cause and effect simultaneously* in the context of *seeds generating manifest activity* and *manifest activity perfuming seeds.*

(3) The meaning of *functioning in tandem with the appropriate consciousness* is that the seeds are continuous in their function without interruption, and that they bring about the continuity of the same qualities

without altering them. If that which we understand as cause disappears before it produces its intended effect, then it has lost its meaning. In order for seeds to function as the causal power for the production of all phenomena, they cannot be something that readily disappears. They must continue without interruption. Seeds, as they bring about the continuity of a certain type over a long period of time, act as *seeds generating seeds,* discussed at length above. By "long period of time" here, we are discussing a period of time lasting until the attainment of the final stage of enlightenment, which will be discussed in chapter 10.

(4) *Having the same karmic quality as their manifestations* means that the seeds are of the same quality as the manifest activities they produce. In other words, wholesome manifest activities are caused by wholesome seeds and unwholesome manifest activities are caused by unwholesome seeds. Thus, the meaning of seeds having the same karmic quality as their manifestations means that the quality of a certain behavior or appearance automatically resonates with the wholesome, unwholesome, or indeterminate karmic moral quality of the seeds that produced it.

Seeds are again used as a metaphor for the latent potentiality to give rise to each thing, and we have repeatedly seen them described as *the potential within the eight consciousnesses to produce an effect.* However, in reality, the establishment of all phenomena is attributable not only directly to these seeds. In order for things to occur, various kinds of conditions must also be present. This is indicated by the fifth connotation, (5) *seeds produce their manifestations only when the necessary associated causes are present.* This is stating that the occurrence of events awaits the assembly of myriad conditions.

Finally, (6) states that *a seed produces its own particular manifestation and no other,* meaning that the seeds naturally bring about effects that are homogeneous with their own character.

At a first look, the implications of numbers (4) and (6) may be hard to distinguish, but they do refer to two distinct aspects. In #4, *having the same karmic quality as their manifestations,* the issue is one of the *karmic character* or *moral quality* of the seed. In condition #6, that of production of its own peculiar manifestation and no other, the problem is one of *type* or *kind.* We tend to end up referring to *all dharmas* as if they were just one set of things, but all of the phenomena that are produced by causes and conditions (known as *conditioned dharmas*) can be broadly categorized into three groups, which include: (1) mental phenomena (including the mind-king and mental factors), (2) material phenomena (called *form dharmas*), and (3) phenomena that can be classified as neither material nor mental (called factors not directly associated with mind; including such things as time, direction, quantity, etc.). In a very general sense, it would not be incorrect to say that seeds are the causes of the production of all dharmas. However, specifically speaking, it is understood that material phenomena are produced from the seeds of form dharmas, and psychological phenomena are produced from the seeds of mind dharmas. This is the meaning of each seed producing its own peculiar manifestation and no other. It is from these conditioned dharmas that our daily life takes its form. When we consider each seed producing its own particular manifestation and no other, we are shown that an "I" cannot be established based solely on a single type of cause. Any phenomenon that is not defined by all six of these conditions cannot be a seed.

Among these six meanings of seeds, I would like here to stress the special importance of the two connotations *production of their manifestations only after the necessary associated causes are present* and *each seed's production of its own peculiar manifestation and no other.* This entails another look at the *four causes and conditions.* From the very start, Buddhism pays great attention to the matter of cause and effect, and within this notion of cause and effect, it places special stress on the notion of causality through a multiplicity of causes and conditions.

In other words, it is impossible to think that all the things that go into the composition of our actual daily lives occur on their own and without due cause. Rather, it is precisely in the midst of a dynamic assembly of manifold causes and conditions that things come into being, while we go about managing our daily lives. Buddhism assumes this way of thinking to be fundamental, and this approach is clarified and elaborated with far greater precision by the Yogācāra notions of *seeds producing their manifestations only after the necessary associated causes are present* and *each seed producing of its own peculiar manifestation and no other.*

Chapter Six: The Deep Self Absorbed in Selfishness: The Latent Area of the Mind

THE MANAS AND ITS OBJECT

We tend to operate under the assumption that our daily lives progress according to our conscious intentions. But these *consciousnesses that discern objects* that handle the management of our daily affairs—i.e., the five consciousnesses of eyes, ears, nose, tongue, and body, as well as the thinking consciousness—do not continue functioning uninterrupted for twenty-four hours a day. We may sit and gaze out a window at a lovely landscape spread out before us, but by simply closing our eyes, we may be in another land, in our imagination. The visual consciousness can be easily shut down, interrupted, and lost.

Likewise, when we fall into a deep sleep, we suspend the function of the sixth consciousness. The mental functions on the surface of the six consciousnesses have interruptions, but we fall asleep every night with the assumption that when we awake, the same "I" as the present "I" will be there in the morning. We do not consciously confirm this assumption each time we awaken, but if serious doubt were cast on the viability of this assumption, it would no doubt be a bit more difficult to fall asleep at night.

When we consider how we *are* able to wake up as essentially the same person each morning, it becomes clear that there needs to be a region of consciousness that binds together the six interruption-prone consciousnesses, and serves as a broad base of support for human existence. The mental region that we are proposing is not something that we can seek and know directly; without the postulation of a latent mental region such as this, we will be unable to account for the totality of human experience. This led the Yogācāras to postulate the *ālaya-vijñāna*.

Śākyamuni, the first historically-recorded teacher of Buddhism to our world, turned his penetrating eye toward human beings and their surrounding natural world and uncovered the two vitally important Buddhist principles of *impermanence of all phenomena* and *selflessness of all phenomena*. The impermanence of all phenomena means that we, and all aspects of the natural world that surround us, are in a constant state of arising, change, and cessation. There is no way that there can be any such thing as a permanent, unchanging essence, and thus the implication of the selflessness of all phenomena.

The Yogācāras, taking this basic Buddhist idea as a basis, continued the search for the most fundamental latent area of mind that would become known as the *ālaya-vijñāna*. Based on the presence of various requisite conditions in this store consciousness, the seeds that follow each other in succession produce manifest phenomena, and those manifest phenomena in turn perfume the *ālaya-vijñāna* with their impressions and dispositions. The chain of such seeds generating manifest activity and manifest activity perfuming seeds serves to create a continually evolving environment.

We enrich our lives by accumulating new experiences daily, and our store consciousness is something that assimilates the impressions of those new experiences into itself one after another. By this we can clearly understand that the *ālaya-vijñāna* is neither unchanging nor substantial.

However, on the other hand, the *ālaya-vijñāna* is something that maintains a series of moments of general similarity in character—the continuity of sameness. Yogācāra Buddhists discerned that in the latent area of this same mind, there was a strong tendency toward the reification of an unchanging essence. The mental function that served to misconstrue the store consciousness to be a firm, unchanging essence (an "I"), was named the *manas*. The Sanskrit term *manas* is interpreted in texts such as the *Cheng weishi lun*[8] to mean *continually examining and assessing*.

It is helpful to be reminded of the previous discussion of the three meanings of store, in the terms (1) *storer* (2) *stored,* and (3) *appropriated store*. The third meaning is that of *an attachment to a self as referent*.

This refers to the eighth consciousness as it is appropriated and attached to as an object by the *manas*. Conversely, the *manas* takes the *ālaya-vijñāna* as its object, and attaches to it as a self constituted by an unchanging essence. In this, the idea of an appropriated store clearly characterizes the relationship between the *ālaya-vijñāna* and the *manas,* wherein we can see that the aspect attached to by the *manas* is an actual characteristic of the *ālaya-vijñāna.* From this perspective then, the meaning of appropriated store is the most important of the three. The origin of all of our confusions lies precisely within this relationship between the *ālaya-vijñāna* and the *manas.*

Of course, the other two connotations are significant, but the special importance of the appropriated store is that it is the basis for what we regard as the distinctively *religious* aspect of Yogācāra. The purpose of Yogācāra is not merely to map out a structure of the mind—to articulate a Buddhist type of psychology. As is the case with basic Buddhist teachings, the purpose of Yogācāra theory is to bring about liberation from suffering, and achieve peace of mind. To this end, the first thing that needs to be clarified is where the root of suffering lies. Within this soteriological inquiry as the main point of its orientation, Yogācāra tries to provide a clear and detailed explanation of the structure of our mind, its dynamic internal and external relationships, as well as its distinct mental functions.

THE SECOND SUBJECTIVE TRANSFORMATION: THE MANAS

The function of the *manas* is to continually turn its eye toward the *ālaya-vijñāna*-as-self, and to attach to it. The *manas* may also be interpreted as "ego-devotion," as this kind of mental functioning naturally brings us to lead our lives in a state of extreme self-centeredness.

Ryōhen (1194–1252) was a Kamakura Period Hossō priest. In a passage found in his *Two-Volume Hossō Extracts,* a classical Japanese introduction to Yogācāra, he describes the *manas* like this:

Always functioning to pollute in the bottom of the minds of ordinary people, even when the prior six minds are pure, I never fail to attach to the distinction between my self and things. The depths of the mind are always being defiled; they come to this state depending upon the *manas.*

Summarizing what we have discussed so far, let's make an initial attempt to identify the main features of the *manas*. The first feature would be that it constitutes a latent region of the mind that is not directly accessible to conscious awareness. The second is that the mental activity of the *manas* is never interrupted—it is always active. Third, its function is to place "I" at the center of any event, rendering one incapable of unbiased views.

It is only through the consciously aware aspects of our minds that we are able to reflect back on ourselves, and try to map out some kind of realistic future. This kind of activity is both wonderful and praiseworthy, as it is possible for us to mature greatly based on the cultivation of such an attitude. Once we have taken such an action, we may think we have delivered a crippling blow to our selfishness. Not so. Our selfishness and self-love are not things that can be cast off so easily—they are extremely tenacious, and embedded in the subconscious level of our mind, known as the *manas*. Yogācāra Buddhism, in striving to see human being through its function in the reality of daily activities, could not but pay close attention to the matter of our selfishness. And such a view could not find its conclusion without the discovery of the *manas,* the source of selfishness and egoism.

The *manas* is always functioning subliminally. Contributing to the progress and enhancement of society is unmistakably a wonderful and wholesome thing, and naturally, it is will be highly evaluated by society. However, inside the person who is striving to cultivate wholesome attitudes and behavior, regardless of the situation, all such activities are defiled by our selfish mind. The passages in the *Two Volume Hossō Extracts* reflect this sentiment.

The notion that the mode of existence of unenlightened regular people is that of deep attachment to self—one that it is deeply rooted in the reification of the ego-notion—is of course a widely held understanding in Buddhism. However, it was up to the Yogācāras to postulate that this attachment was based in a deep region of the mind called the *manas* and to clearly articulate its characteristics. It is this attachment to self that Buddhist practices aim to remove.

Please note here that within representative bodhisattva practices of Mahāyāna Buddhism, such as the six *pāramitā*s ("six transcendent practices")[9] and the *four methods of winning people over,*[10] the act of *donation* is always at the top of the list. The action of giving things over to others, especially when there is no expectation of recompense, is intimately connected to the removal of attachment to self. Donation, especially in this Buddhist sense, involves giving one's own possessions to others unconditionally—without any expectation or subsequent regret. To whatever extent we continue to lead our lives permeated by an attitude of ego attachment, we are to that degree incapable of freely and unconditionally offering our own possessions to others.

Concerning the practice of donation, there has been, from an early period of Buddhism, a teaching called the *three rings ("practices") of purity*. The three rings are those of the donor, the donee, and the offering. When the three are carried out completely without any hint of internal struggle, it is regarded as a perfect donation—an unconditional form of donation where one does not expect as much as a single word of thanks. We might call it "giving and letting go."

On the other hand, conditional donation is called the *three impure rings*. Here, self-centeredness is not only not abandoned; the prejudice to the self is of immediate importance and attention. When we first begin to practice donation, all of our offerings are contaminated by this quality, as the practice of donation is always bound with those things that are offered, and because the self, as the focus of our awareness, makes it extremely difficult to carry out donation in the unattached mode of the three pure rings. However, it is precisely because of this that it is considered to be such an important practice in Buddhism.

If we think about this problem of donation while bearing in mind that this *manas* sinks subliminally, secretly, and deeply into to self-attachment, we cannot but know that our "giving" is something that is done, regardless of the situation, only at our own convenience.

It is easy to see how selfishness cannot but bring great influence to bear upon the objects that we see, hear, and consider. Previously, we have seen in the discussion of the *ālaya-vijñāna as the first subjective transformation* that the object of cognition is first transformed as it is contextualized by the totality of our own experiences. Now, on top of this, we imbue greater significance to objects of our cognition according to the self-centeredness emanating from the *manas*. We are conducting our lives in an environment that is subjectively altered by the *ālaya-vijñāna,* and is now, in addition, subjectively altered by the *manas.* This is called the manas as the *second subjective transformation.*

We live our lives based on the assumption that we directly perceive, and are accurately interpreting, objects with a fair amount of accuracy. Since we naturally assume that we are apprehending objects of cognition as best as possible, it does not occur to us that we are purposely twisting the object before our eyes to fit our own convenience.

Instead, we take as our objects of cognition things that have already been influenced and altered by the *ālaya-vijñāna* and *manas* consciousnesses. Everything has been greatly twisted and defined to support our own convenience, and as such, objects of cognition are in fact *referents that have been transformed* by the *subjectively transforming minds.* The things that we are cognizing are certainly not "external objects" in the commonly understood sense of the term. Those of us who believe we are carrying out our daily lives based on an accurate understanding of the true way of being should begin to abandon that conceit and begin to rethink the matter just a bit. This realization forms a critical juncture in Yogācāra teaching.

THE FOUR AFFLICTIONS OF THE MANAS

While the *ālaya-vijñāna* accumulates all of our actions and behaviors and has the character of *continuity of sameness,* or, *changing but unchanging,* the *manas* misconstrues the *ālaya-vijñāna* to be an invariable, substantial thing identified as the self, and tenaciously attaches itself to it.

The perfuming of the impressions of every single one of our actions into the *ālaya-vijñāna* happens subtly, below the threshold of our conscious awareness. At the same time, the attachment to this *ālaya-vijñāna* by the *manas* is not directly knowable. Therefore the elimination of the self-attachment of the *manas,* the internal egoism and selfishness held within the "I," is impossible simply by making a conscious decision to do so. Within the conscious "I" that earnestly reflects on the selfishness of one's speech and behavior, there is a subtler "I" that is sunken deeply in egoism. From here, let us consider the actual mental functions of the *manas* comprising the roots of egoism and selfishness.

Yogācāra Buddhism says that we possess a total of fifty-one mental functions, and it divides these factors up into six groups: *omnipresent, object-contingent, wholesome, primary afflictions, secondary afflictions,* and *indeterminate.* These six groups were presented earlier in chapter 3, as itemized in Vasubandhu's *Lucid Introduction to the One Hundred Dharmas.* Within these mental factors, all except for the omnipresent factors are concentrated in the *manas* as *afflictions* and *secondary afflictions.* These are the factors that have in common the characteristic of bringing us irritation and suffering.

Primary afflictions contain the fundamental afflictions, or mental disturbances, representing the fundamental psychological functions that make our mind and body suffer intensely. Within this group are the six mental factors: *craving, ill-will, pride, ignorance, doubt,* and *incorrect* views. Among these, those understood to be functions of the *manas* are *craving, pride, ignorance,* and *incorrect views.*

The *Lucid Introduction to the One Hundred Dharmas* is thought to have been written by Vasubandhu at a point when his Yogācāra thinking had reached maturity, but there is another famous earlier work by Vasubandhu which is even more influential, the *Triṃśikā* (translated into Chinese with the title "Thirty Verses on Consciousness-only"). In this text, four afflictions are associated with the *manas*: self-delusion, self-view, self-conceit,[11] and self-love.

If we compare these two texts, despite the fact that the order of the itemization is different, we can see that their understanding of mental functioning is the same. However, one passage from the *Triṃśikā* states that "[the *manas*] always acts in tandem with four afflictions: self-delusion, self-view, self-conceit, and self-attachment," and has been repeatedly cited since early in the history of Yogācāra studies. It makes sense, then, to use the passage from the *Triṃśikā* as the main source for our discussion of these afflictions. If we properly understand these four afflictions associated with the *manas* in the *Triṃśikā*, self-delusion, self-view, self-conceit, and self-love, they can been seen as analogous to the ignorance, incorrect view, pride, and craving of the *Lucid Introduction to the One Hundred Dharmas* respectively.

The mental factor of self-delusion, synonymous with such Buddhist concepts as *ignorance* or *bewilderment* (Skt. *avidyā, moha*), refers to the obscuration of reality, and implies a state of confusion. Because it is the psychological function that serves as the source of all afflictions, self-delusion is considered to be the most original, fundamental, aberrant mental function. It is the prime cause for the confusion that we experience in our daily lives.

In addition to its function in the *manas,* self-delusion is also understood to operate throughout the prior five consciousnesses and the sixth, thinking consciousness. Despite the seemingly simple label *ignorance,* the true scope of its function is various and indeterminate. Within this, in its role as a factor in the psychological functioning of the *manas,* its distinguishing characteristics are the fact that it arises concomitantly with self-views, self-conceit, and self-attachment, as well as the fact that it has continued to function since the immemorial past without interruption. This indicates delusion in regard to the principle of no-self, which corresponds to the *self-view* (the next item to be discussed), and is rightly called *self-delusion.*

The rubric of *incorrect views* is subdivided to five kinds of content:

(1) the view of a composite self,
(2) extreme views,
(3) perverse views,
(4) attachment to one's own views, and
(5) views of attachment to moral discipline.

Self-view corresponds to the *view of a composite self,* and refers to the misconstrual of the "I", which is established as an aggregate of various elements to act as an invariable essence. Self-view means that one sees the "I" to be a real self, when in fact it is impermanent and lacking an inherent essence. We continually operate in the midst of a wide variety of mistaken views, all of which have their roots in this self-view.

To properly understand incorrect view, we need to recall the mental factor of *intelligence* that was listed in the group of object-contingent factors that were introduced in chapter 3, "The Functions of the Mind." Intelligence is a mental function that chooses, distinguishes, and determines the object of cognition. It operates not only in a wholesome manner, but also unwholesomely and with karmic moral indeterminacy. When intelligence operates in an unwholesome manner, by grasping things in a distorted way, it is known as *incorrect view*.

Incorrect view is understood to operate within both the thinking consciousness *(mano-vijñāna)* and the *manas* consciousness. Above, when we broke down the incorrect view into five specific aspects, we stated that the view of a composite self was roughly analogous to the self-view among the four afflictions. More precisely speaking, within the view of a composite self there is an inherent aspect that functions at all times without interruption, and this is the self-view of the *manas*. All the functions occurring within the view of a composite self that are subject to interruption (as well as extreme view, perverse view, attachment to one's own view, and view of attachment to discipline) are understood not as functions of the *manas* but as being the psychological functions of the sixth, thinking consciousness. Extreme view, perverse view, attachment to one's own view, and the various views of attachment to discipline all ignore the principle of cause and effect, and refer to mistaken and potentially harmful non-Buddhist teachings. Except for extreme views, these views are not innate, but are the result of cultural conditioning from the time of birth. The innate, latent mental function that notices the store consciousness' character of continuous sameness but takes it to be an unchanging essence—thus imputing a true self—is the self-view within the four afflictions.

Self-conceit is a mental activity wherein one takes great pride in oneself and looks down on others. Generally the term *conceit* refers to a mental function that is generated based on a comparison between oneself and others, wherein one's own worth is exaggerated to generate the feeling of superiority.

Self-conceit is distinguished into seven types of manifestations, called the *seven kinds of conceit*:

(1) basic conceit,
(2) conceit in regarding oneself as superior to equals and equal to superiors,
(3) conceit in feeling superior to manifest superiors;
(4) self-conceit,
(5) conceit in superior knowledge,

(6) conceit in regarding oneself as only slightly inferior to those
who far surpass oneself,

(7) conceit in regarding oneself as possessing virtues, such as wisdom and enlightenment, while actually lacking them.

The seven kinds of conceit refer to psychological functions that origi-
nate in the course of comparison between oneself and others, and which
motivate the cultivation of a greater feeling of superiority. An interesting
example is seen in that of *conceit in regarding oneself as only slightly inferior
to those who far surpass oneself.* This is a self-conceit that rears its ugly head
when we encounter a person who is superior to ourselves in every aspect.
One might well assume that in this sort of circumstance no form of conceit would arise whatsoever, since there is no recourse but to admit that
other party is excellent. But even a slightly adjusted acknowledgment, such
as "I might not be quite as good as him, but I'm definitely on the right
track," causes us to rationalize that the other person is only a little bit better than ourselves.

In this case, to our regret, we are unable to exercise a pleasant feeling of
superiority, and so instead we try to minimize the feeling of inferiority we
may experience. Conceit in regarding oneself as only slightly inferior to
those who far surpass oneself is not an obvious form of conceit, but it well
shows the incredibly subtle face of the basic function of conceit.

Conceit is understood to be a mental factor operating in both the sixth
and seventh consciousnesses. The self-conceit that operates within the limits of the thinking consciousness can be noticed in self-reflection, and thus
suppressed. However, forms of conceit that operate within the *manas* are
functioning in the subconscious region of the mind, so that no matter how
earnestly one reflects, one can never come close to influencing or manipu-
lating them.

To believe one thoroughly knows things of which one is actually igno-
rant is called *conceit in superior knowledge*. By deeply reflecting on this
shortcoming, we can experience a marvelous advance in our spiritual
progress and greatly develop our lives henceforth. However, Yogācāra
Buddhism holds that beneath the functioning of this surface mind there
is an unremitting mental function of conceit, which secretly relies on the

fictitious self and serves to generate a feeling of contempt for others. This is none other than the mental function of *self-conceit* found in the *manas*.

Self-love is also called self-craving, craving, or addiction. Craving is a mental factor that attracts us toward whatever object we find appealing. Craving, along with ill-will and folly, is counted as one of the three poisonous afflictions. Craving is a well-known mental function that is one of the most fundamental factors serving to pull us ever further from the state of buddhahood. Yogācāra Buddhism sees the mental factor of craving as operating broadly, being seen in the prior five consciousnesses, the thinking consciousness, and the *manas*. Within this self-love, the *manas* misconstrues the *ālaya-vijñāna* to be a real self and firmly attaches to it, such that our awareness of the attachment will eventually come to the fore. We can enhance this awareness by reflecting on our words and actions.

In the case of craving, it can only be identified as operating at the external level of the *mano-vijñāna* (thinking consciousness). At that time, the self-love of the *manas* is still writhing beneath the surface of the thinking consciousness.

THE EIGHT SECONDARY AFFLICTIONS OF THE MANAS

As we have seen in the prior section, the *manas* misconstrues the continuity in type of the deep *ālaya-vijñāna* and considers it to be a true self, and then attaches to it incessantly. It has as its representative functions the four primary afflictions of self-delusion, self-view, self-conceit, and self-love, which are always concomitant with it. When the final two afflictions of *ill-will* and *doubt* are added to these four, we have the full set of six primary afflictions, the fundamental mental disturbances that are the source of other derivative troubles.

Based on these fundamental afflictions, a set of derivative afflictions, known as the twenty secondary afflictions, are stimulated. Among this group are eight psychological functions understood as being associated with the *manas*. These are: *no faith, indolence, self-indulgence, depression, agitation, forgetfulness, incorrect knowing,* and *distraction*. When afflicted states of mind *(kliṣṭa-manas)* arise, all eight of these mental factors arise in tandem. Defiled mental states disturb our mind, and as a result the distance between us and buddhahood becomes steadily greater.

Let's take a brief look at these eight mental factors from among the *secondary afflictions*.

No faith (Skt. *aśraddha*) is a term that defines the lack of inclination to be concerned with wholesome dharmas, of entrusting oneself to them, and of looking forward to their positive effects. *Wholesome dharmas* are the positive spiritual mental functions, and the action of no faith defiles our minds. Faith is a fundamental Buddhist concept that implies the power we have to purify our minds and move us closer to our goal of buddhahood. Since *no faith* is a mental function that interrupts the establishment of faith within us, it is something that defiles our minds and interrupts our spiritual path.

Most directly induced by no-faith is the mental factor of *indolence* (Skt. *kausīdya*), the lack of any motivation toward the cultivation of wholesome dharmas. It is a psychological function that represses the motivation toward honest improvement, causing Ryōhen to write: "Those who lack faith are indolent; those who are indolent lack faith."[12]

Buddhist practices are commonly summarized under the rubric of "eliminating the unwholesome, cultivating the wholesome." This implies the elimination of mental disturbances and the maintenance of the energy to proceed toward buddhahood, which can be interpreted as simply drawing a clear line between what one will do and what one will not do. Unless we set a clear line between what we will and will not do, we cannot establish any clear principle of living. Living a life without principles, just following one's desires wherever they may lead, leads to a life filled with *self-indulgence*. This further leads to a greater defilement of the mind, and the positive factors that may have been previously been assimilated into the "I" are corrupted.

Depression is a psychological condition where the mind sinks, preventing one from properly identifying and judging things and events. The counterpart of this condition is the mental factor of agitation, a psychological condition where one's mind abnormally rises and floats. The main symptom of this mental factor is the inability to thoroughly ascertain the character of things.

Forgetfulness (Skt. *smṛti-nāśa*) stands in contrast to the mindfulness of the object-contingent factors. If in losing the focus of attention one also loses sight of the object of cognition, it is not possible to adequately assess it, or contemplate upon it. As a result, one's mind becomes scattered. Forgetfulness is considered to be the main contributing factor to distraction.

Distraction works counter to the object-dependent mental factor of *concentration*. Rather than focusing the mind on a single object, one's attention jumps, moves, and wanders from thing to thing, one after another. As a result, one tends to develop imbalanced and mistaken views.

At first glance, *distraction* and *agitation* may seem to refer to the same sort of condition. But whereas in the former state one's mind jumps from one object to another, agitation refers to the tendency of the mind to make contact with a single object in an odd way, leading to confusion.

The last of this group, *incorrect cognition* is a mental function wherein a mistaken understanding is made regarding all knowable objects.

Since the function of the *manas* is deep, subtle, and not directly knowable, the same thing can be said about its four basic afflictions. Therefore, the explanation of the treatment of mental factors that are concomitant with the *manas* is usually carried out in the context of discussions of the *thinking consciousness*. Although we have explained these factors here as clearly identifiable functions, in actuality they should be understood as ineffable factors, simply being muddying, vague psychological functions.

SUMMARY

We are told that the Buddha never grew weary of deepening his personal realization of the impermanence of all phenomena and teaching others about the selflessness of all dharmas. Buddhists in later generations may well interpret the Buddha's energy as coming from a desire to transmit these truths to those who are so distant from him in time and space. But this is really nothing more than our own interpretation, made from our own perspective. The real source of his motivation was simply that such notions as impermanence and no-self are really quite difficult to grasp for people who live in such a deep state of confusion. Thus, there can be no doubt that it was precisely in response to this difficulty that Śākyamuni was motivated to re-explain such seminal concepts again and again.

Human beings and the natural world that surrounds them are all in a state of movement and change, and those things that exist here and now are nothing more than provisional combinations of various elements. Nothing is changeless and substantial, and this is the meaning of the impermanence of all phenomena and the selflessness of all dharmas. Such truths are presented to us in the hope that we might at least tentatively allow for the fact that they might turn out to be true.

At the same time, even though we talk about impermanence we cannot but directly feel that there is something about the "I" of today and the "I" of several months ago that has remained constant, hardly changing throughout time and growth. Being attracted by this *unchanging* aspect, we understand it to be something substantial connected with the self, and our attachment to this substantial, unchanging aspect continues throughout the rest of our lives as our de facto state of being.

Concerning this mechanism of attachment to a fictitious self, Yogācāra Buddhism created a detailed elaboration of this latent mind of self-attachment called the *manas* that takes the *ālaya-vijñāna* as its object. Since our attachment to a fictitious self is understood by the fact that the *ālaya-vijñāna,* which accumulates the impressions of our actions and creates a general sense of continuity in type from the past to the future, is misconstrued by the *manas* to be an unchanging substantial self.

Eishun, wanting to express this human impermanence and the selflessness that it is derived from, composed the following verse:

> The old and the young all know they are going to die, and say so as
> if they really know it. But even though they say so, they really don't
> know what's going to happen.[13]

By attaching strongly to our egos, we exhibit our own lack of awareness of the real nature of our own existence. It is painful. I can hear the sigh of lamentation from Eishun.

The *manas* is a mind preoccupied entirely with self-interest, and since we possess this mind deep within us, we are, every moment of every day, inevitably self-centered. We twist and turn in the direction of self-concern and self-benefit in every circumstance that befalls us.

The mental factors of the primary and secondary afflictions present in the *manas* are, as we have seen above, not only associated with the *manas,* but also with the *mano-vijñāna,* or, according to the situation, even within the prior five consciousnesses. The psychological functions of the primary and secondary afflictions that work at the level of the sixth consciousness allow us to be conscious, and therefore when engaged in deep and sustained reflection, we are able to suppress them to a certain degree, but not the four afflictions of the *manas.* The four afflictions are continuing in their subtle, subliminal function, which means that our efforts at conscious reflection can only take place fragmentarily, sitting atop a base permeated entirely with self-centeredness.

Of course, by attempting to work toward a positive direction at the level of consciousness, we may bring great meaning to our lives. However, in our deep self there are four afflictions that do not rest in their attachment to the fictitious self. Truly, it is as Ryōhen said:

Always functioning to pollute in the bottom of the minds of ordinary people, even when the prior six minds are pure, I never fail to attach to the distinction between my self and things. The depths of the mind are always being defiled.

This is why our efforts at cultivating wholesome behavior cannot be clearly and immediately effective.

The deep mind that is absorbed in self-centeredness pulls into it the objects considered good and convenient according to its bias, and focuses exclusively on these as the objects of its cognition. This is another vitally important way for us to realize that objects do not appear to us as they really are, but in a state that is subjectively transformed by the selfishly oriented *manas.*

Chapter Seven: The Variously Assessing Mind

THE DEEP MIND AND THE THINKING CONSCIOUSNESS (*MANO-VIJÑĀNA*)

In the course of our daily lives, we meet many people, see and hear various things, and make an effort to experience everything. Our lives consist of a series of relationships between the "I" and these people, things, and events. But the content of these relationships is going to depend greatly upon the way in which we cognize these things. We know that at the earliest point in the cognitive process the *ālaya-vijñāna*—the first subjective transformation representing the collected array of all our past experiences—greatly imbues its influence onto the cognitive object. The *manas,* the second subjective transformation, then attempts to understand each thing with unfathomable self-centeredness. The ground of our daily cognitive life lies in the deep mind of the *ālaya-vijñāna,* constituted by the whole of our actions and experiences, along with the mind of attachment to the self, known as the *manas.* These are the cognitive foundations from which we experience our lives. Although we believe that we live in a fully conscious and aware manner, upon taking full account of the cognitive process and its inevitable passage through these prior two transformations, it becomes difficult to maintain the view that we conduct our lives *only* through our conscious awareness.

Given the fact that these first and second subjective transformations occur subliminally, we do not have conscious access to them, and as a result have no idea what is actually going on in the depth of our minds. Its function is truly quite mysterious—especially that of the *ālaya-vijñāna,* the most fundamental, psychological base that undergoes beginningless perfuming. Since the *ālaya-vijñāna* is constituted by the entirety of our past experiences, it is something that we can trace back infinitely into the past. Who knows what might be stored within it? All that we can say with any certainty is that it is far beyond anything we might be able to imagine—that it is nothing short of a total mystery. We may be convinced that we are carrying out our lives in a state of manifest conscious awareness, but underneath everything lies a profoundly unknowable psychological basis.

The relationship between the consciously aware region of the mind and the deep, unfathomable region reminds me of a story that I read of a man who dreamt of a giant eggplant. When asked how large it was, the man replied, saying, "It was like attaching a calyx (the cup-like base found on vegetables like eggplants) to the dark void." In this story, the darkness extends to infinity, and so this eggplant is infinitely large. The *ālaya-vijñāna* is comparable to the infinite darkness of the eggplant, and the superficial thinking consciousness is like the calyx attached to its tip.

Although the metaphor of an eggplant calyx for the consciously aware mind is a bit of an oversimplification, hopefully it serves to show the limitations of the *mano-vijñāna* in accounting for the totality of our lived experience. Since the thinking consciousness is subject to interruptions, that which is gained through the mental functions such as perception, feelings, thinking, and intentions cannot be a full account of reality. Yet despite the fact that these breaks lead our psychological functions to be noncontinuous, we are nonetheless living unified and continuous lives. This can only be possible because of the existence of the *ālaya-vijñāna* that sustains the surface mind, extending into the infinite past. The *ālaya-vijñāna* is seen as the indescribable, vast, psychological base of our lives when compared to the surface mind of the sixth, thinking consciousnesses.

But this does not mean that we should regard the conscious mind as being insignificant. There is no other way to engage in self-reflection than through our conscious awareness, which allows us to adjust to our present situation and discern the path that we need to tread into the future. Without relying on the psychological functions of the sixth consciousness, there is nothing we can do to improve ourselves. Even though the domain of the thinking consciousness receives profound influence from the deep mental regions of the *ālaya-vijñāna* and *manas,* our ability to learn from experiences and progress into the future is only made possible by the thinking consciousness in the present moment.

I would like to quote the opening passage of the short story "Swiss Chard"[14] as a metaphor for the relationship between the deep mind and the sixth consciousness.

> His wife's voice was heard, saying, "it is just like the congealing of the bean curd (tofu). When the soybeans have just been ground, there is nothing but soupy, amorphous, soybean pulp, and there is nothing that can be gotten from the mix. However, after the bittern is mixed in, the parts that end up becoming bean curd clump together, becoming clear and firm, and that which will become bean curd and that which will not are clearly distinguished."
>
> "No matter what, bittern is necessary," came the voice of Mr. Yoichi from the main house. "That's right. If you don't use it, the bean curd will never take shape," said the wife and Mr. Yoichi, soberly, together as one voice.

The function of the deep mind is to continuously maintain the impressions and disposition of past experiences in the form of seeds without any loss. This can be seen as the original framework of individuality, but it would be more proper to call it a "formless original form." So let's imagine the deep mind as something like the soupy, mixed soybean pulp as seen in the above story.

No matter how flawless the deep mind may be in terms of what it receives and preserves, based only on an awareness of its function as receptacle, it is not possible to identify a clearly defined and distinct "I." Just as the form of bean curd can only be obtained after bittern is put into the soupy soybean pulp, on top of the formless, soupy "I," it is only after the appearance of the thinking consciousness, which assesses each separate thing, that a distinct, individual "I" is formed for the first time.

In comparing the conscious mind to the calyx of the eggplant, we drew attention to the fact that just like the bittern that congeals the bean curd, this consciousness is vitally important. While understanding the store consciousness as the basis of existence, if there is no function of conscious awareness, that which we call "I" has no medium to function in society. Thus, while Yogācāra Buddhism is primarily known for its extensive investigations into the operations of the subconscious regions of the mind, the thinking consciousness also has vitally important implications.

Religion is inevitably something that demands *faith,* or belief from us. Given the variety of forms of religion, it is natural that definitions of faith are also various. One interpretation, based on our discussion thus far, is to say that faith involves the sincere taking of our entire past as a foundation while simultaneously looking forward to the creation of a bright future. While this is a somewhat narrow perspective of the notion of faith, it reflects at least two essential points. One is that no one can rearrange his or her past. Whatever may be in our past, we have to accept it. The second point is that the thinking consciousness is operating while being continually subjected to the powerful influences of the *manas.* Even the wholesome mental factors are working under the severe constraints of a deeply embedded selfish attachment that is utterly bereft of the ability to take an unbiased perspective on anything.

The only recourse we have is to consciously accept our past without a struggle, and from the position of leverage provided by this awareness, elevate, deepen, and broaden our inclination toward the world of the Buddha. This is the first religious step of Yogācāra, its foundational form of faith.

THE THIRD SUBJECTIVE TRANSFORMATION: THE SIXTH, THINKING CONSCIOUSNESS

Our mind does not simply cognize objects exactly as they exist in themselves. On the contrary, it is fundamentally disposed to subjectively alter everything that is seen, heard, and touched. Our minds carry out such subjective transformations at three levels. The first two of these three levels, as we have already seen, are the *ālaya-vijñāna* and the *manas.* The first subjective transformation is made against the backdrop of the gamut of our prior experiences, and the second subjective transformation is motivated by our deeply-held attachment to ourselves. Even though both of these dramatically alter the objects of cognition, we operate under the assumption that these objects are being directly cognized, and we go forth with our lives based on this.

Once we understand this teaching, we can no longer continue assuming that we are cognizing things as they really exist. Still, the simple intellectual understanding of this fact is of no consequence if some concrete action is not taken to stop this habitual tendency. And if nothing is done to counteract it, we become ever more strongly convinced that our own view is basically correct instead of finding liberation from the habit. This may lead us to wonder how we can ever hope to attain a correct perspective.

The process of subjective alteration does not stop with the first and second subjective transformations. There is now yet another subjective transformation occurring in addition to these, known as the third subjective transformation. In the context of the mind-kings of the eight consciousnesses, this refers to the operation of the sixth consciousness and prior five consciousnesses. The case of the prior five consciousnesses will be discussed in further detail in the next chapter.

Yogācāra Buddhism broke down our psychological functions into fifty-one mental factors, which were then classified into six groups according to their character. These six groups of factors are:

(1) omnipresent factors,
(2) object contingent factors,
(3) wholesome factors,
(4) primary afflictive factors,
(5) secondary afflictive factors, and
(6) indeterminate factors.

It is understood that the fifty-one mental factors are directly associated with the thinking consciousness, and that the thinking consciousness has an extremely wide range of varying, psychological functions.

One implication of this is that at the level of conscious awareness, the mind is capable of working in either wholesome or unwholesome modes. While undergoing the powerful influences of the subliminal *ālaya-vijñāna* and *manas,* and according to the variety of psychological functions carried out by the thinking consciousness, we may either come closer to buddhahood, or fall further away from it. Based on the function of this sixth consciousness, things are subjectively altered, and these transformed objects are taken to be the objects of our direct cognition. This third subjective transformation begins when we create understandings regarding objects based on this.

One of the most commonly-seen ways of distinguishing the general functions of the human mind is to break it down into the three aspects of cognition, emotion, and intention. Some schema simplify it even further, into the two general aspects of cognition and emotion. These approaches have been taken since ancient times, and are not necessarily Eastern or Western in origin. In Yogācāra, the thinking consciousness is usually analyzed into the three aspects of cognition, emotion, and intention, and from these three categories opens up a wide range of topics for discussion. We can see from this that the third subjective transformation is quite complex in terms of its content.

The most important factor to take into account when discussing the third subjective transformation is that objects of observation will differ significantly from person to person, depending on personal interests and attitude—and there is an unlimited range of possible interests and attitudes. One might have a readily apparent and strong awareness of a certain matter, and go on to pursue it deeply. One may also have some level of concern for an object but no impetus to pursue it. Even though both kinds of concern are for the same object, the character of what ends up being perceived can differ immensely. Thus, the former person sees much that is not seen by the latter, whose volitional requisites toward the object's intellectual appeal that would lead one to study more deeply are sparse. The latter person does not see what the former person has apprehended through greater application of attention.

In the case of a deficiency in apprehension for something that should be normally cognized by the thinking consciousness, we can see the operation of the factors of *slackness* from among the *secondary afflictions,* or *drowsiness* from among the *uncategorized* factors, which bring dullness to one's cognitive faculties and gloom to one's emotional state. For example, we may be able to read the text on the page of a book, but with this slackness we may not be able to understand the content of the paragraphs—the sentences written on the page are nothing but individual letters conveying no meaning. Or, in the case of *ill-will* among the afflictions, the psychological function of anger narrows our overall cognitive scope. As a result, our ability to execute proper judgment is lost. Thus the emotive elements of the thinking consciousness carry out significant subjective alteration of the object of cognition.

THE VARIETIES OF CONSCIOUSNESS

On an early summer morning before dawn, a man stands in a garden. Catching the familiar smell of the lotus blossoms, he forgets the suffering of last night's poor sleep due to the heat of the summer night, as if it never occurred. During this time the sky lightens gradually, and lotus flowers of various colors—white, red, and spotted purple, gradually show their neat appearance. He brings his face close to the flower of a nearby white lotus, and breathes in its scent deeply. At this time, the visual consciousness and the olfactory consciousness of prior five consciousnesses work first, perceiving that it is a white, fragrant lotus. He experiences the direct perception of that thing, simply as it is.

Arising at the same time as the function of the prior five consciousnesses is the sixth consciousness. This thinking consciousness *(mano-vijñāna)* takes the sensation by the prior five consciousnesses to the level of conceptualizing that "this is a beautiful white, lotus flower, which smells very good." And perhaps the cognition is even brought to the level of comparison, in such thoughts as "the wind orchid and the flowers of the allspice tree also smell good, but after all, the lotus is the best."

However, the thinking consciousness does not require the function of the prior five consciousnesses in order to operate. The prior five consciousnesses are limited in their function to direct sensory experience, and thus to a specific location, and to the direct sensation of a presently existent object. But the thinking consciousness can, for example, reflect on the lotus flower that was enjoyed this morning, and in the course of ruminating on it, make various conjectures, comparisons, associations, and forecasts, all without experiencing a concrete object. To reflect this meaning, the thinking consciousness is also referred to by the connotative technical term *consciousness with a wide range of referents.*

The cases of the arising of the thinking consciousness are broadly categorized into two types: (1) those where it arises in tandem with (at least one of) the five sense consciousnesses, and (2) those where it arises unassociated with them.

In the first case, the thinking consciousness operates concomitantly with the sense consciousnesses and enables them to more precisely cognize the sensory object. It is quite normal for us to use our sense consciousnesses and thinking consciousnesses in tandem when various conjectures and intentions are experienced together with sensory perceptions. In this circumstance, the thinking consciousness that arises in tandem with the sense consciousnesses is distinguished into two further types: (a) the thinking consciousness that has the same referents as the sense consciousness, and (b) the thinking consciousness that does not have the same referents.

In contrast to this thinking consciousness that arises in tandem with the sense consciousnesses is (2) the thinking consciousness that arises unassociated with the sense consciousnesses. This form of consciousness is further distinguished into: (a) the thinking consciousness that arises subsequently to the sense consciousnesses, and (b) the thinking consciousness arises independently of the sense consciousnesses. The thinking consciousness that arises subsequently refers to the case where after the operation of one of the sense consciousnesses, the object is taken up by the thinking consciousness. This function is not simultaneous with that of the five sense consciousnesses, but occurs in their wake.

Let us again take up the example of reading a book. First the visual consciousness sees the printed characters on the page just as they are. Then the thinking consciousness that had arisen simultaneously with the visual consciousness follows, cognizing the meaning of the words. However, it does not stop there, as we continue to relate to the contents of what has been read, pondering its meaning. This is the function of the thinking consciousness following upon the operation of the sense consciousnesses.

There is also the case where sentences and words are recalled only upon a certain occasion. Remembering the words of a favorite poem or novel, we ruminate on their meanings, savoring them more deeply. This kind of function of the thinking consciousness does not occur simultaneously with the prior five consciousnesses, nor does it directly follow upon them.

In a poem entitled "Thinking of Kōfukuji Temple," Shūsō Dōjin (Aizu Yaichi) wrote:

> I guess that spring is has come; many people are coming and
>   going;
> In the buddha-garden, perhaps the flowers are blooming.

Dōjin, who had returned to Tokyo, was writing a verse of yearning. Within the compound of the Kōfukuji Temple in Nara, the people, while waiting for spring, are coming and going in a relaxed manner. Dōjin never actually witnessed this scene with his own eyes, but his independently arising thinking consciousness, based on his past experiences, imagined that around now, there must be such a scene occurring in Nara. And so he placed himself quietly into this scene.

If the only role of the thinking consciousness was to respond to cognitive objects appearing before our eyes, our lives would end up being pretty boring. It is the ability to pull things out of the depths of our own being, examine and contemplate their individual characters, and then accumulate this knowledge that brings richness and depth to our lives. This is the indispensable function of the independently arising thinking consciousness.

The Mind That Assesses Variously

Yogācāra Buddhism analyzed our mental functions including the five omnipresent factors, the five object contingent factors, the ten wholesome factors, the six fundamental afflictions, the twenty secondary afflictions, and the four uncategorized factors, for a total of fifty-one, which were categorized into six groups. The ability of these fifty-one to function is due mainly to the sixth, thinking consciousness.

The thinking consciousness, possessing these fifty-one psychological functions and capable of cognizing all dharmas, surveys the wide range of objects covered by these functions and allows us to make a variety of assessments regarding them. Since mental factors having a clearly defined karmic moral character—such as the wholesome factors, afflictions, and secondary afflictions—operate within the thinking consciousness, our conscious awareness is capable of leading us in either wholesome or unwholesome directions.

Even though wholesome functions are available to us, such functions must operate on top of the deep selfishness of the *manas* as expressed in its four concomitant afflictions. This puts us in the position of swimming upstream, as it were. Here we are again reminded of Ryōhen's admonishment: Even at the time when the six minds are functioning purely, we are always being defiled in the depths of our consciousnesses. While this may be so, it is a clear, unmistakable fact that within ourselves we possess the basic provisions for the practice of a wholesome, spiritual life, and the ability to strive for enlightenment. Having realized this special characteristic of the thinking consciousness, we can begin to control the mental functions of the primary and secondary afflictions. Once the goodness in the mind has been solidified, this turns into a great basis which we utilize to further ourselves toward enlightenment. We can either take a powerful first step in the direction of the good, or further enhance disturbances of the mind, scattering body and mind in a thousand pieces, telling everyone that we were forced into this situation by external circumstances beyond our control. The decision regarding our course of action is entirely up to our own conscious mental activity.

In chapter 3 ("The Functions of the Mind") we discussed the four mental factors subsumed under the categories of *omnipresent, object-contingent,* and *uncategorized.* Then, in chapter 6 ("The Deep Self Absorbed in Selfishness") we surveyed the four mental factors of craving, conceit, ignorance, and incorrect views from among the primary afflictions, as well as no-faith, indolence, dissipation, slackness, agitation, forgetfulness, incorrect knowing, and distraction from among the secondary afflictions. We now move to covering the remaining two basic afflictions, and then follow up with the remaining twelve secondary afflictions, and finally finish with the eleven wholesome mental factors.

The mental factor of *ill-will* is an affliction related to anger. It is usually described alongside craving and ignorance, under the label "the three poisonous afflictions," as introduced earlier. These three are considered to be the most rudimentary of our psychological problems. Jōkei (Gedatsu Shōnin; 1155–1213), when describing the condition of man while engaged in the process of deep self-examination (in the *Anthology of Rousing the Mind from Delusion*), calls us "fellows deeply impregnated with poisonous habituation."[15] His statement reminds us that we are nothing but beings who lead our lives under the profound influence of the impregnation by the karmic impressions in our *ālaya-vijñāna,* which is in turn conditioned by the rudimentary psychological functions of craving, ill-will, and ignorance.

We have already seen the mental factor of *craving,* wherein one covets without limit those things that are pleasurable. The opposite of this is the mental factor of *ill-will,* a psychological function of anger and hatred directed toward the things that one does not appreciate. Once anger arises, any amount of peace and equanimity of body and mind that one may have maintained up to that point is immediately lost.

Doubt is a psychological function only found in the sixth consciousness. When one has misgivings about the validity of such principles as the law of cause and effect and no-self, hesitation prohibits us from fully entrusting ourselves wholly to these basic truths.

The next ten mental factors from the secondary afflictions, including anger, resentment, worry, concealing, deceit, flattery, arrogance, envy, hostility, and parsimony, are all functions found only in the domain of the thinking consciousness.

Anger is a feeling of indignation toward those things that are disagreeable to oneself. Once this mental factor arises, uncouth speech and behavior are sure to ensue.

Resentment is the psychological function that occurs based on the continued function of anger, and is characterized by feelings of abhorrence and grudge toward that which does not suit one's own feelings. As a result of this function, our mental and physical equanimity is ruined.

Worry is a psychological function that occurs with the extended experience of anger and resentment, where one repeatedly feels indignation and a sense of grudge. The mind is not peaceful, and in this state of confusion, one is antagonized by everything he sees or hears, bringing about automatic, intense suffering. Needless to say, these three secondary afflictions of anger, resentment, and worry all arise based on the fundamental affliction of ill-will.

In Buddhism, our intense desire for worldly reputation, gain, and profit is considered to be a very fundamental problem. The mental factors of concealing, deceit, and flattery are all the mental functions that derive from attaching too much importance to fame and wealth, and are understood to be indicative of deluded thinking. Therefore, it is understood that these three mental factors are derived from the combination of the fundamental afflictions of craving and ignorance.

Concealing occurs when one fears losing the social reputation that one has created because people will discover mistaken or evil actions and behavior. People often go to great lengths to hide those activities that, if known, will diminish their position, and these actions lead only to further anxiety and worry.

Deceit occurs when greed causes one to try to achieve fame and profit by deceiving others, pretending to have abilities that one does not. *Flattery* is a similar psychological function operating in concern over fame and profit, causing one to excessively praise someone else under false pretenses.

Next, *arrogance* is a feeling of conceit that we experience when we attach too much importance to our talent and property, which we find to be superior in comparison with those of others. It is considered to be a manifestation of the fundamental affliction of craving.

Hostility is a mental state wherein there is a total lack of pity for all things, which allows one to proceed to inflict pain upon others without remorse.

Envy occurs when one does nothing but worry over reputation and wealth, and becomes annoyed at seeing the success and honor attained by others, giving rise to envy and jealousy. When someone around us does some good work that is positively evaluated by society, we calmly say, "isn't it great?" However, if someone advances rapidly without any discernible effort, we are bothered. Here the mental function of envy has become activated. *Hostility* and *envy* are considered to be derivatives of the fundamental affliction of ill-will.

Parsimony is the mental function of being stingy in regard to one's possessions, whether they be material things or one's knowledge. Needless to say, this function is based on the fundamental affliction of *craving*.

This concludes the discussion of the mental factors of the secondary afflictions that are unique to the thinking consciousness. We now move to those that are not necessarily relegated to the thinking consciousness.

Unscrupulousness is a state of mind bereft of self-reflection, a true lack of any sense of shame, while *shamelessness* similarly refers to a lack of concern about what others may think. It is thought that these two mental factors lurk without fail in the bottom of our minds when we are in an unwholesome psychological condition. In addition to functioning in the sixth consciousness, they are thought to operate within the five sense consciousnesses.

Let us now look at the wholesome mental factors.

Faith is a purifying mental function, which in Yogācāra Buddhism is distinguished into three aspects: (1) cognitive faith, (2) joyous faith, and (3) faith as the intent to cultivate wholesome dharmas.

Cognitive faith is the effort to try to deeply ascertain the truth of the world. This is a function based on the mental factor of *devoted interest* (*adhimukti*; one of the *object-contingent* factors), meaning a deep understanding. It can be said that cognitive faith is a noetic function because it seeks to achieve a deep understanding of phenomena.

Joyous faith is the movement of the mind wherein one attempts to devote oneself toward seeking enlightenment. Most of the time when the term faith is used in Buddhist texts by itself, it is this aspect which is being indicated. This can be considered the emotional aspect of faith.

The faith of seeking to cultivate wholesome dharmas means that one strongly intends to cultivate and to consummate all forms of goodness. This is considered to be a function of the will.

The mental function of faith is generally understood as being rooted in the emotional aspect of the human mind. However, the act of believing in Buddhism is not something limited to the realm of the emotions. Within the mental functions of faith there is actually the inclusion of all three human aspects of cognition, emotion, and volition, and thus the distinction of faith into these three aspects. Faith is a mental activity that mobilizes all elements possessed by human beings, to thrust us forward into a life based on truth.

Buddhism is commonly characterized as a lifestyle that focuses on eliminating evil and cultivating goodness. The psychological function of single-mindedly acting according to the truth, and living a life based on reality, is called *zeal*. When this mental state is functioning, the attitude of dullness and gloom toward creating truth and goodness (the mental factor of *laziness* among the secondary afflictions) is severed. The mental factor of wholesome desire that acts in the direction of goodness serves as the basis for the psychological function of zeal, which has has already been fully discussed above.

Conscience refers to the power of one's continuous self-reflection in the context of the teachings that one has entrusted oneself to, while one's sense of *shame* functions contingent upon one's actions being observed by the people that surround one. Utilizing both, one tries to work diligently toward the eventual attainment of the life of truth while continually adjusting one's own behavior. We can say that conscience refers to a decision to take a certain course of action based on one's own inner principles, while the sense of shame takes the principles of society as a moral standard. When we aim ourselves in a wholesome direction, we begin to reflect deeply on our own daily life while holding a healthy respect for true teachings. However, at the same time, we should not fail to acknowledge that we are being observed by others. For the "I" who exists nowhere else than within society, to take advantage of being able to be purified by the relationship with this society is more than simply appropriate—it is quite honorable.

The three factors of *no craving, no ill-will,* and *no folly* are mental states wherein one does not covet, does not get angry, and is not deluded; three mental functions that act to subdue the three poisonous afflictions of craving, ill-will, and ignorance. These are called the *three wholesome roots*. These three are the foundation for the emergence of all forms of goodness. In the same way that the size of a plant's growth is dependent upon the quality of its roots, the three good roots of no craving, no ill-will, and no folly impact our progress toward enlightenment.

No folly indicates that one has a clear understanding that all things arise, abide, and disappear according to such principles as the impermanence of all phenomena and the lack of self in all dharmas. Of course, it is not assumed that we have already attained full mastery of the way of thinking based in impermanence and selflessness.

By establishing our thinking based on such truths and making an effort to make this thinking as the basis for our daily lives, we will be able to subdue the feelings of craving toward remembered objects of attachment, gaining control over feelings of detestation toward those things that we abhor. These are the roles of the mental factors of *no craving,* and no *ill-will.*

Pliancy is a psychological function that separates the mind from the afflictions that trouble it, causing the mind and body to feel light and relaxed. It is a function that counteracts the mental factor of *slackness* of the secondary afflictions. Distinguished from the other wholesome mental factors, it is considered to be a mental factor seen only in deep states of meditative concentration, and is not often encountered during our daily lives.

The next three mental factors of *diligence, indifference,* and *non-hostility* can be understood as reflecting the necessary attitudes that we need to develop for the cultivation of goodness.

Diligence refers to the mental function of working hard without any laziness, actualizing all kinds of goodness and drawing a clear line of distinction between good and evil. Of course one can benefit from having diligence in any sort of endeavor, but in the context of the Buddhist path, if one is indolent, one has no chance of catching the hand extended from the world of the buddhas.

Being diligent in the practice of goodness should not be seen as a drudgery—in fact, it can be enjoyable and fulfilling. However, if one is diligent to excess, it can turn into the mental factor of *agitation* of the secondary afflictions, and end up resulting in extreme instability and defeating the whole purpose. To prevent this, goodness is something that is to be developed calmly and steadily. This attitude of calmness in regard to the attainment of one's goal is known as *indifference.* It is difficult, but our goal must be to practice goodness while severing ourselves from any notions of attaining it. Diligence and indifference are derived from a combination of the psychological functions of *zeal* and the three good roots.

On the other hand, *non-hostility* is a part of the psychological function of no ill-will. When, for example, we are faced with a person we disagree with, he is not to be taken as an object of hatred. One rather feels empathy with the person, fully understanding the pain of the afflictions that he is holding within himself.

Here we have treated the main features of the wholesome mental factors only in a very cursory manner. In Yogācāra Buddhism it is said that when the wholesome mental factors are arisen, all ten, except for pliancy, function in unison. Since the wholesome psychological functions work in tandem like this, when the wholesome functions are operating in the thinking consciousness, we exert a powerful positive influence on the subconscious mind of ego-attachment, progressing ourselves toward enlightenment.

SUMMARY: THE PROBLEM IS, WHAT TO DO NOW

We know that the sixth consciousness, as the consciousness with a wide variety of referents, is a mind that can take any given thing to be its cognitive object, during past, present, and future, and can support both wholesome and unwholesome functions. The thinking consciousness is a mind that can assess each separate phenomenon in a wide variety of ways.

Even though the thinking consciousness can carry out a variety of assessments, it is still nonetheless a relatively superficial form of mind, with its psychological functions strongly subject to the influences of the *ālaya-vijñāna* and *manas*. We can never discuss any kind of a real "I" in the present while ignoring our past activities and behaviors, or our profound attachment to the imputed self.

Nonetheless, we still have the capability of saying to ourselves "this isn't a good idea," and from this moment forth, begin to recreate ourselves as new beings. *Indolence* is transformed into *diligence,* and *laziness* is turned into *zeal.* The reason for the possibility of this change is that the basis of our existence—the *ālaya-vijñāna*—has an indeterminate character that is neither good nor evil. Despite the fact that our present self has been created from our past activities and experiences, the past is still the past. We are now actively creating a future that has a different quality from this past, and it will be the focus of our experience henceforth.

Despite the length of time we have been exercising excellent wholesome mental functions and seeking to become one with enlightenment, we should never imagine that we can receive a moment of rest from our endeavor. Our thinking consciousness is endowed with both wholesome and afflictive factors, and conflicting psychological functions are always working within us. We live with the potential to tend toward either a good or evil direction at any time. Our daily life can be seen as something carried out within the tug-of-war between goodness and affliction, putting us in a position to never find peace. In the sixth consciousness, wholesome trends change into afflictions in the flash of a moment. Because we are trying to learn from these subtle points and reach the realm of liberation, it is necessary that we focus on our target. In the *Tale of the Vegetable Roots* (Ch. *Caigen tan*), we learn that:

When mind and body are luminous, a clear sky pervades, even in a dark room. When our thoughts are dark and dim, vengeful demons inhabit the bright light of day.

Usaburo Imai's translation differs slightly, but also clarifies the thought: "When body and mind are shining brightly, even in a dark room, the clear sky is visible; when our feelings are darkened by mundane thoughts, we are caught by demons in the middle of the day." The term "dark room" can be interpreted in various ways, but I take it as the condition of our insecurities in society and their recognition of us, and our inability to accept this state of affairs. If the character of the mind is luminous at such a time, the person is unrestricted and need not be sick at heart. "Body and mind are luminous" describes the state wherein we have decided on a clear and firm purpose for our lives. When someone lacks a goal, wherever he may be, he won't shine. Conduct your daily life with a specific aim or purpose. In this, the environment created by the rising up of the wholesome mental functions will automatically open up immensely.

Human beings all have the ability to realistically reflect on themselves and seek mental equanimity, and to actively avoid indolence and craving. If we steadily handle our lives in this way, though it may take time, we will certainly be thrust upward to the world of the Buddha. This is the core principle of Yogācāra Buddhism.

Chapter Eight: The Function of the Five Senses

COGNITION IN THE PRIOR FIVE CONSCIOUSNESSES

Within the mind-king of the eight consciousnesses, the six consciousnesses (visual, auditory, olfactory, gustatory, tactile, and thinking) are generically known as the *consciousnesses that discern objects*. This is because these six consciousnesses, in contrast to the *ālaya-vijñāna* and *manas,* have the ability to discern and discriminate objects of cognition. Within these abilities there is understood to be a function of subjective transformation of the cognitive object, and this is the third subjective transformation.

In this chapter, we will look at the five consciousnesses: The visual consciousness, the auditory consciousness, the olfactory consciousness, the gustatory consciousness, and the tactile consciousness, which correspond to seeing, hearing, sense of smell, taste, and the sense of touch respectively. When these are compared with the thinking consciousness, their mental activity can be seen as being relatively simple. Together, they are usually referred to as the five prior consciousnesses, which can be understood as a general rubric for the function of the five senses.

Each of the prior five consciousnesses respectively cognizes its own kind of corresponding object: material objects, sounds, odors, tastes, and tactile sensory objects. The visual consciousness sees the color, shape, and the condition of a given thing; the auditory consciousness hears various sounds; the olfactory consciousness smells the difference between pleasing fragrances and bad odors; the gustatory consciousness tastes the things that are put in the mouth, discerning whether they are bitter or sweet, and the tactile consciousness identifies the things (tactile objects) that touch the skin as being, cold, warm, hard, soft, wet, or dry. The sense consciousnesses only apprehend their designated objects.

The primary function of these five consciousnesses is to perceive the given object as it is. There is no further linguistically-based interpretation carried out, such as "this is a flower" or "this is magnificent scenery." They only receive things as they are directly sensed, without conceptual overlay. This kind of cognition is called *direct perception.*

Buddhist logicians understand that there are generally three methods for the cognition of things, which are: (1) direct perception *(pratyakṣa-pramāṇa)*, the unmistaken direct perception of things; (2) inference *(anumāna-pramāṇa)*, to know things through their logical connections, such as through discrimination and comparison, and (3) mistaken perception *(apramāṇa)*, which refers to erroneous function of either of the prior two. The prior five consciousnesses and the eighth consciousness operate only with direct perception, while the seventh consciousness operates with mistaken perception. The situation of the sixth consciousness is of course more complex, since its basic function is to first guess randomly about each thing and deepen the cognition while making a comparative investigation. Hence it frequently makes mistakes. And, since the thinking consciousness also works through the mode of direct perception, this means that it functions through all three modes of direct perception, inference, and mistaken perception. When compared with the broad range of functioning of the sixth consciousness, the prior five consciousnesses function with relative simplicity.

The second feature of prior five consciousnesses is that they only perceive objects that are in the present, and are as such limited by the given scene. The prior five consciousnesses cannot retrace the past or mull over the future as can the thinking consciousness. They can do nothing but directly sense the object that is before them. If one's eyes are shut, the visual consciousness ceases to function. These interruptions constitute a prominent feature of the prior five consciousnesses.

Because the prior five consciousnesses are sensory cognitions, the function of discriminating the object is done through the particular sense organ. This sense organ is called "faculty" (Skt. *indriya*), which denotes the possession of creative power, a metaphor based on the energy seen in the roots of plants and trees, enabling them to grow and develop and instill life into their trunks and branches. The five consciousnesses take as their bases of support the five faculties, and through them make direct contact with their respective objects. The sensory organs, or faculties, are seen as possessing not merely passive, receptive capabilities, but more importantly, generative powers comparable to that seen in the roots of plants. Depending on the visual faculty as its root, the visual consciousness can function aptly to cognize its material objects.

Yogācāra analyses indicate that these faculties are distinguished into the two aspects of the physical sense organ and the supra-physical sensory abilities. The physical sense organ contains the tangible-visible, eyes, ears, nose, tongue, and skin, while the supra-physical sensory ability is the sensory power contained within the given sense organ.

We are inherently endowed with these faculties, but they are distinct abilities and are unique to every sentient being. For instance, it is said that the sense of smell possessed by dogs is about 6,000 times as strong as that of human beings. While walking with its master on the same road, the degree of a dog's awareness of the world through its olfactory consciousness is vastly incomparable to that of its master. By comparison, our sense of smell is drastically limited in its ability to reveal the character of any given object based on its odor. Sensory function is categorized as the direct perception of things as they are in themselves, but naturally there are limitations to be seen in the prior five consciousnesses, based on biological conditions.

We are, from the beginning, beings subject to the restrictions of biological conditions. We cannot discern ultraviolet and infrared rays with the naked eye, despite the fact that they certainly surround us everywhere. The mind of the visual consciousness can do nothing more than delimit color and shape, and within the confines of that delimitation, cognize, through direct sensation, the objects of the visual realm. Even within the same species of human being, there are persons who can detect extremely subtle differences in the notes of the musical scale, as well as persons utterly incapable of such acute sensory awareness. Even though the same notes are being played on a piano, according to the individual conditions of the sensory ability of the listeners, the auditory object is not the same. Thus, the prior five consciousnesses, according to the individual and biological conditions of their five sense faculties, first undertake the subjective transformation of the five objects.

THE PRIOR FIVE CONSCIOUSNESS AND THE SIXTH THINKING CONSCIOUSNESS

We have now roughly identified some features of the prior five consciousnesses. However, their most important single characteristic is that they must operate in tandem with the sixth consciousness. They cannot function independently without it.

If the ramifications of this are considered from the perspective of the prior five consciousnesses, we see that the five senses are subject to the strong influences of the thinking consciousness. Taking as an example the function of the visual consciousness, we assume that we see the vast scenery spread out before our eyes as it is, and that there is nothing else to be apprehended. But the actual function of our seeing things is not so simple. The thinking consciousness is directly involved, and this visual consciousness that is subject to the influences of the thinking consciousness in turn subjectively transforms the objects that it sees.

There is an interesting example in the case of making stone-prints, a technique where one places a piece of rice paper over an old tile and then presses down on the paper with a wet towel so that it fully and directly adheres to the tile. After it has dried slightly, one taps lightly with a *tanpo*[16] smeared with India ink, and the impression from the tile is copied into the paper. The resulting piece of art is something that has quite an interesting shape, and once the technique is learned, many people become obsessed with this as a hobby, wanting to make stone prints of anything they can find that has an uneven surface.

When a stone print is taken, one comes to feel as if the material of the stone-print is leaping into our eyes from the other side. This is because up until the time the person learned the technique, most of the things that one has seen have undergone the subjective transformation based on the background of one's habituated field of vision, and as a result other significant aspects of the object had gone unnoticed. Because the result of this revised subjective transformation is so outstanding, we suddenly take notice and are reinvigorated in our sensory perception. In this way, the prior five consciousnesses of the sensory functions are also able to subjectively transform their objects.

We should also note that since the prior five consciousnesses are senses, they are unable to distinguish between good or evil in terms of karmic moral character. However, since it is the case that they function in tandem with the thinking consciousness, it is almost inevitable for them to come under the influence of the character of that consciousness at any given moment, and thus the prior five consciousnesses can become wholesome, unwholesome, or indeterminate in karmic moral quality.

When we give rise to the mental function of craving at the level of the thinking consciousness, the function of the prior five consciousnesses is strongly influenced by this, and they will take on its character. This is best shown in the expression "to look at something with great desire," which we may interpret by saying that the eye consciousness is under the powerful influence of the sixth consciousness, and this quality becomes infused into the visual faculty that is the container of this consciousness.

In summary, it is understood that the psychological functions of these prior five consciousnesses include: the five mental factors of *omnipresent factors*, the five mental factors of *object-contingent*, all eleven wholesome mental factors, the three mental factors of *craving, ill-will,* and *ignorance (folly)* among the afflictions, the ten mental factors of *shamelessness, unscrupulousness, agitation, slackness, no faith, laziness, indolence, forgetfulness, distraction,* and *incorrect knowing* of the *secondary afflictions,* in total, thirty-four.

Chapter Nine: Who Am I?

THE MEANING OF "BECOMING BUDDHA"

We have now come to learn something about the structure of the mind and its functions, and how to distinguish between wholesome and unwholesome using subjective transformations of the three regions of the mind, through the functions of the eight consciousness mind-king.

Let us briefly recap those points. First of all, the *ālaya-vijñāna,* in accumulating the impression-dispositions of our actions, takes a powerfully influential role in the overall function of the eyes that see people and things. Our past influences the present and, naturally, imprints anything we do. This is the deep mind of the *ālaya-vijñāna.* Next, this *ālaya-vijñāna* flows as the continued succession of sameness from the distant past up to the present. We begin to feel and take hold of a reified, unchanging self within this *ālaya-vijñāna* and we become strongly attached to it, acting in a self-centered manner. This is the mental activity of the *manas.* Yogācāra Buddhism understands that the four afflictions of craving, conceit, ignorance, and incorrect views are always at work in the mind's innermost depths as the specific mental activities of this *manas.*

Knowing this, we understand that our present life is continually subject to the strong influence of two subconscious elements: the accumulation of our past activities and experiences, and selfishness guided by deep attachment to an ego. However, it is also pointed out that based on the influence coming from wholesome mental factors found in the thinking consciousness, we are provided with access to a means of awakening to, and becoming intimate with, the Buddha's teaching. This is possible because the *ālaya-vijñāna,* as the psychological base of our life, has the special characteristic of bringing causes to their fruition in a state of karmic moral neutrality.

Gaining familiarity with the Buddhist teachings, we begin to develop the growing clarity of an aim of enlightenment in our lifetimes, the goal of buddhahood. Saying that one will someday arrive to the buddha realm can be paraphrased by saying that one day, the realm of the buddhas will be directly manifested within my very self. Fixing one's sight on enlightenment, and living one's daily life with that goal as a guiding light, is considered walking on the Buddhist path. One's eventual arrival to the state of enlightenment is called "becoming Buddha."

"Becoming Buddha" means that if we make an effort to truly understand the structure and mechanism of our own minds along with its various psychological functions, and endeavor to nurture wholesome psychological functions while trying to subdue the afflictive mental factors, somewhere at the other end of this path, the buddha-state will manifest itself. The consummation of this buddha-state is precisely the meaning of "becoming Buddha."

But with this understanding, a question arises regarding the certainty of enlightenment as our final goal. Simply this: Can "I" really become a Buddha, or not? Even though the "I" has been deeply and wonderfully moved by the Buddha's teachings, is it really possible for this "I" to become a buddha? This is something that we cannot but be greatly concerned with, and thus I would like to take it up as the topic of discussion in this chapter.

ALL SENTIENT BEINGS POSSESS THE BUDDHA-NATURE AND THE DISTINCTIONS IN FIVE NATURES

The central theme for all branches of Buddhism is how to overcome suffering and eventually be freed from it. By now, we understand that the marrow of the teaching is that which we saw in the content of Śākyamuni's first sermon delivered at Deer Park in Benares, where he discussed the *Four Noble Truths* and *Noble Eightfold Path*.

Since the Four Truths and Noble Eightfold Path were introduced in chapter 5, I will not re-explain them here, but simply reiterate the fact that

Buddhism takes the Four Noble Truths as its point of departure, aiming to bring human beings, who rush manically from the suffering of pain to the suffering of pleasure, to a state of liberation. We who yearn for the world of Buddha, and who take the various teachings delivered by the Buddha as our great guiding light, single-mindedly desire to trace the way back to the realm of peace and equanimity.

Within Mahāyāna Buddhism, all sentient beings are understood as possessing a noble quality that is fundamentally equal to, and connected to, that of the Buddha. It commonly stated in many Mahāyāna scriptures, most notably the *Nirvāṇa Sūtra,* that "all sentient beings possess the buddha-nature," or "each and every sentient being will become a buddha." Seen in the context of the *Nirvāṇa Sūtra,* this phrase refers to the possibility of becoming Buddha. Moreover, the idea that each and every sentient being will become a buddha means that all living things can *equally* become buddhas. Among the various schools of Mahāyāna Buddhism, this general way of thinking is associated with a specific doctrine, called One Vehicle Buddhism, which is a strongly idealistic approach to the understanding of the Buddhist doctrine.

The idea that everyone possesses the ability to become a buddha serves to encourage our interest in the notion of enlightenment. Indeed, there is no other teaching that will lead us to be as intimate with the Buddhist teachings and give rise to the will to walk the Buddha's path. We are greatly stimulated by this noble ideal, becoming steadily more encouraged to deepen, heighten, and broaden our own practice of Buddhism.

Yogācāra Buddhism takes a considerably different standpoint from other Mahāyāna Buddhist schools on this point—a considerably more realistic approach. The notion that all beings possess the buddha-nature is understood as an ideal that all practitioners should continuously orient themselves toward. But Yogācāra argues that in terms of actual practice, such an attainment is almost impossible, and goes on to state that there is a type of sentient being who cannot attain buddhahood.

This may startle some. Buddhism is a religion that invites us to reach for liberation, and directly bring us there. Because Yogācāra Buddhism—in particular, East Asian manifestations known as Faxiang (Chinese), Yusik (Korean), and Hossō (Japanese)—taught that there were beings incapable of becoming buddha, they ended up getting into heated disputes with the One Vehicle schools, a complication we will elaborate upon further below.

When we consider the broad range of sentient beings, even without their variations in external form and appearance, we must acknowledge that they internally contain a wide variety of differences in terms of ability and character. In roughly defining a Buddhist lifestyle, I would like to think of it as the lifestyle of consistent application toward the elimination of evil and cultivation of good, with the ultimate aim of liberating our mind, while simultaneously caring for others. But we certainly cannot say that all sentient beings are endowed with the same capacity for the elimination of evil and cultivation of goodness. Beyond these very general differences, the Yogācāras understood that all living beings do not uniformly become buddhas in the same way, and furthermore, that the state that they attain differs according to their predilections. They differentiated between three paths to the attainment of liberation, called the *śrāvaka* vehicle ("path of direct disciples"), the *pratyekabuddha* vehicle ("path of adepts who achieve enlightenment based on their own effort and insights"), and the bodhisattva vehicle ("path of enlightened practitioners who prioritize the well-being of others over their own attainments"). In contrast to the One Vehicle Buddhism that promised the attainment of buddhahood by all beings, the Yogācāra school is known as Three Vehicle Buddhism.

Yogācāra Buddhism established a theory of classification of sentient beings into five categories of distinctive proclivities:

(1) sentient beings with a nature predisposed for *śrāvaka* practices
(2) sentient beings with a nature predisposed for *pratyekabuddha* practices
(3) sentient beings with a nature predisposed for bodhisattva practices
(4) sentient beings with an indeterminate nature, and
(5) sentient beings lacking the nature (potential) for liberation (known as *icchantikas*).

Among these, the nature predisposed for bodhisattva practices refers to practitioners who possess the character that enables them, via the removal of both afflictive and cognitive hindrances, to attain to a state of liberation equivalent to the buddhas. "Liberation" is understood to have two different aspects, known as *nirvāṇa* (extinction of suffering) and *bodhi* (enlightened wisdom). It is said that nirvāṇa and bodhi were both attained by the Buddha upon enlightenment. *Nirvāṇa* refers to the state of peace attained in mind and body, whereas *bodhi* refers to true wisdom.

We carry out our lives assuming ourselves to be something substantial and unchanging, and we become deeply attach to this assumed self (this attachment is known in Sanskrit as *ātma-grāha*). But we attach to more than simply a notion of a self. We also reify the things that we see, hear, and think, into substances, and attach to them as well. This is called *attachment to dharmas* (Skt. *dharma-grāha*). Among these two attachments, it may be the case that we can earnestly reflect and bring ourselves to the awareness of our attachment to self, making an effort to avoid it. But attachment to dharmas occurs at such a subtle level that stemming it based on conscious reflective awareness is practically impossible for most people. We grasp at all dharmas (all phenomena), despite the fact that they are nothing more than a provisional combination of elements according to certain conditions. Taking these as the framework created from our past experiences, along with accordance to our individual circumstances, we see, hear, and think. When we regard the content of such seeing, hearing, and thinking to be accurate, attachment to dharmas ends up being far more difficult to come to reconcile than attachment to self. How do you deal with something that is virtually unnoticeable? This attachment to dharmas engenders the *cognitive hindrances (jñeya-āvaraṇa)*, while attachment to self engenders the *afflictive hindrances (kleśa-āvaraṇa)*. Nirvāṇa is said to manifest based on the removal of the afflictive hindrances, while bodhi is obtained by the elimination of the cognitive hindrances.

The practitioner with the potential for bodhisattva practices is a person who is originally endowed with a proclivity for overcoming the two obstacles of afflictive and cognitive character. If these proclivities are developed, a practitioner can certainly attain buddhahood.

By contrast, practitioners whose natures are either predisposed for *śrāvaka* practices or predisposed for *pratyekabuddha* practices are only endowed with the proclivity to sever the afflictive hindrances. These two types of people are distinguished from each other in that the practitioner with the nature predisposed for *śrāvaka* practices must receive the teaching from a buddha, other eminent teacher, or comrades and friends, after which he can eventually walk the Buddhist path, while the practitioner with the nature predisposed for *pratyekabuddha* practices is a person who overcomes the afflictive hindrances based on his or her own effort and insights, without needing to rely on teachers and comrades.[17]

Based on their exertion of effort, practitioners of these two types are said to be capable of completely severing the attachment to self. They have the potential to manifest a certain type of liberation, but that form of liberation is radically different in quality from the perfect enlightenment experienced by the Buddha.

Next, the indeterminate nature summarizes a class of practitioners who are simultaneously endowed with a combination of two or more kinds of natures among the above-mentioned *śrāvakas, pratyekabuddhas,* and bodhisattvas, who have not determined the course along which they will traverse. Within this indeterminate nature there are four different types of combinations:

(1) the nature that is not determined between the two of *śrāvaka* and bodhisattva;

(2) the nature that is not determined between the two of *pratyekabuddha* and bodhisattva;

(3) the nature that is not determined between the three of *śrāvaka, pratyekabuddha,* and bodhisattva, and

(4) the nature that is not determined between the two of *śrāvaka* and *pratyekabuddha.*

Among these, only the first three groups contain the bodhisattva nature, and thus the proclivity for eliminating both kinds of hindrances of afflictive and cognitive, and are able to proceed toward an enlightenment equal to that of the buddhas.

Finally, sentient beings lacking the nature for liberation *(icchantikas)* are a class that cannot achieve liberation through all eternity because they lack the capacity to sever even the afflictive hindrances, not to mention the cognitive hindrances. Living a life with their light smothered by the attachment to self and to dharmas, they lack the potential for liberation. However, by virtue of some conducive conditions, along with some knowledge of the Buddhist teachings, they may adjust their ways somewhat and gain some degree of control over their lives.

This kind of division in type refers to one's spiritual predisposition, or the character that one is born with. In the Yogācāra context, this is a condition related to *innate seeds* (see the discussion on innate seeds and newly perfumed seeds in chapter 5, "The Production of Things"). Because practitioners with the nature to overcome both the afflictive hindrances and cognitive hindrances possess an undefiled character destined for liberation, their nature is said to be constituted by inherently uncontaminated seeds.

The doctrine of distinction in five natures asserts that when liberation is achieved, its content differs according to whether or not one is endowed with the seeds of *śrāvaka*-hood, *pratyekabuddha*-hood, or the uncontaminated seeds of the bodhisattva in the eighth consciousness. Among living beings, there are some who can never attain any sort of liberation.

One of the most surprising aspects of this doctrine of distinction in five natures is its clearly stated declaration that some sentient beings lack the potential for liberation. While it was not the original intention of the Yogācāras to harshly single out a specific group, it is only realistic to note that there are those who, having spent a long time sunk deeply in delusion, cannot manifest liberation despite their positive actions. Thus they are said to lack the potential for liberation.

Although the One Vehicle Buddhists who advocate the attainment of buddhahood by all sentient beings do not claim that this designation of a class of sentient beings lacking enlightenment potential is an outright heresy, they do categorize it as an *expedient* teaching—with the implications of "expedient" being that of inferiority. But this simple categorization as "expedient Mahāyāna" leaves us in an unsettled situation, which has generated significant debate since an early period.

One of these debates took place during the third year of the Ōwa period (963), when Ryōgen of the Tendai Sect of single vehicle Buddhism and Chūsan of Kōfukuji Temple debated over the interpretation of the line contained in the second chapter of the *Lotus Sūtra* which says: "among those who hear my dharma there are none who do not become buddhas."

Considered to be a pivotal phrase in the *Lotus Sūtra* discussing expedient means, it was understood as establishing the position that all sentient beings become buddhas. Ryōgen, in his attack of Hossō Buddhism, cited this phrase from the *Lotus Sūtra* as his trump card, declaring that Yogācāra held a deviant Buddhist position. In doing so, he interpreted the passage as such: "If there are people who hear my dharma, not one of them will not become a buddha." However, in his response to Ryōgen, Chūsan of Kōfukuji Temple reinterpreted the scriptural passage to read: "Even if there is someone who does hear my dharma, the one lacking the nature will not accomplish buddhahood."

To be fair, Chūsan's rendering of this line is rather forced. It does, nonetheless, provide one example of how to interpret the Buddha's teaching—by taking the position that all sentient beings accomplish buddhahood, or holding to the distinction in five natures—was the subject of repeated debate. In the days subsequent to this sectarian Ōwa debate, both sides declared victory.[18]

This disparity in view between all sentient beings becoming Buddha and distinction in five natures is grounded in the difference between an idealistic point of view and a realistic point of view. To the extent that members of each side attach to their own positions, they will accomplish nothing more than continuing to traverse along parallel lines, and we can never expect any satisfactory resolution of the controversy. However, those of us who are trying to follow the Buddhist path should, regardless of the standpoint, be willing to give serious consideration to the perspectives of others.

SENTIENT BEINGS LACKING THE NATURE FOR BUDDHAHOOD

In general, all schools of Mahāyāna Buddhism agree that all sentient beings possess the buddha-nature—that all sentient beings become buddhas. When our interest in Buddhism is initially sparked, or when we arouse a clear determination to seek enlightenment, this idea serves for us as a great unmistakable voice of encouragement which helps lift us up toward our goal. We are strongly encouraged by such phrases as "all sentient beings possess the buddha-nature" or "each and every sentient being becomes a buddha." Our interest in Buddhism is increasingly stimulated, and our determination for the goal of enlightenment is steadily strengthened. This idea that each and every sentient being becomes a buddha points to an ideal we can actively pursue, and something that we can use to encourage others.

However, this may become difficult when we consider that the prospect of all things manifesting liberation equally is untenable, and furthermore, that there are sentient beings lacking the nature for liberation. Admittedly, this is an unusual doctrine. However, we should remember to never take the division into five natures as either a standard by which others are measured in the Buddha-path, or as a teaching that coldly divides practitioners into classes. The theory of the distinction in five natures is something that should be taken up only in the context of one's own self-examination regarding one's own qualities.

Buddhist Practice

Throughout this book, we have touched briefly here and there on matters related to defining the Buddhist's life on the path, or faith. From the beginning these have been little more than clumsy attempts, so I would like once again here, in reflecting on the actualities of practicing the Buddhist Way, to summarize with the following two main points.

The first is that no matter what, Buddhist practice must be based on the repeated examination of one's past activities. But if this examination is not carried out through a clearly defined principle, then it will end up being nothing more than a bit of indulgence in one's memories, which does no one any good. Instead, without falling into self-recrimination, we should strive to examine ourselves using knowledge learned in the teachings of Buddhist scriptures. It will be at that time that we first experience a Buddhist form of self-reflection. The second essential point is that while taking this kind of sincere reflection, we create and develop a way of living our lives henceforth, remembering the Buddhist teachings and committing to them as a way of bettering ourselves. But from the perspective of sentient beings lacking the nature for liberation, how do we do this?

The previous statement, that "all beings possess the same nature of accomplishing buddhahood," points out that all living things can achieve liberation equal to that of the Buddha. What other feeling could we have, aside from utter joy, at hearing this proclamation? We are strongly encouraged by such a feeling, and almost naturally our interest in enlightenment is amplified, and pure feelings toward liberation grow in strength.

Though we may be charmed or encouraged by this notion, how shall we go about accumulating the virtues of self-examination, and how shall we reflect on the course we have taken to arrive at this point?

"Self-examination" implies the realistic observation of the self. This is very easy to say, but since the task of observing the self implies the observation of something that lacks any form, if there is not some sort of method for conducting this observation, it will bear no fruit. This is exactly what led to the construction of the extremely detailed organization of the mind and the list of various psychological functions provided by Yogācāra. As a result, a composite of eight consciousnesses was articulated, made up of the surface minds of the prior five consciousnesses and the sixth consciousness, which undergo the strong influence of the deep minds of the eighth, *ālaya-vijñāna,* and the seventh, *manas,* consciousnesses. Moreover, as we have already seen, the fifty-one psychological functions were classified and analyzed in detail as the six groups of factors including omnipresent, object-contingent, wholesome, primary afflictions, secondary afflictions, and uncategorized. By utilizing this framework to help us shed light on the chain of our daily behavior, we might come to see our true selves.

On the other hand, by conducting such self-examination through this kind of framework, we may fear that that which is uncovered will be too disgusting to gaze upon. With this thought, our feelings of elation cannot but fade away, and we gradually slide in gloom and fear of what may be discovered in this self-examination.

But the number of Buddhist teachings is vast, and the content and meaning of each has a wide range of varieties and permutations. By focusing on consolidated sets of practice, such as the six *pāramitā*s (donation, observation of the precepts, forbearance, zeal, meditative concentration, and wisdom) and *four methods of winning people over* (donation, kind words, altruistic activity, and working together with others), we find a stimulating, engaging method of self-examination and Buddhist practice. A buddha is a person who fully cultivates these items to their final fruition.

However, in the case of the six *pāramitā*s alone, the content of even a single item can vastly mushroom. For instance, donation is practiced in the context of the three rings of purity, and only assumes its full meaning when it is done selflessly and without regret. While we may offer our possessions and knowledge to the people around us, we in fact attach to our act of giving, and further exacerbate our devotion to our own self. Our daily life normally functions in the context of giving and receiving, and although we may donate regularly, this ends up becoming a major factor in the furtherance of our attachment to self. For those of us so deeply attached to our lives, or to ourselves, donation done according to the principles of the three rings of purity is, honestly speaking, something far too large, far too deep, and far too difficult to be fully carried out. Within the three rings are contained the ramifications that when someone comes to beg from us, we completely offer up our very own existence. It is a process that demands perfect and entire commitment.

If we take into consideration such statements as "all sentient beings possess the buddha-nature" and "each and every sentient being accomplishes buddhahood," from this perspective of those encountering the very first challenging practices of the *pāramitā*s, who in the world can be so bold as to proclaim "I have the buddha-nature within me"? We instead begin to feel as if we are the one who is *furthest* from the buddha-realm—a disheartening conclusion, to say the least.

Though we are encouraged by the Buddhist expression "all sentient beings possess the buddha-nature," and may rejoice at knowing that we may eventually arrive to the state of buddhahood, on the other hand if I reflect on and examine the "I" who is supposed to arrive to this state of buddhahood, it seems impossible. There is a considerable gap here, between this declaration of the possession of buddha-nature and what I actually see in myself based on rigorous self-reflection. How did earlier Yogācāra masters perceive and address this problem?

Jōkei resolutely studied the psychological factors that compose the mind according to Yogācāra, and used them to earnestly examine himself. His descriptions of the experience state that:

> If I desire to enter the vast and great entrance to the mind, my
> nature is not equal to the task.
> If I want to practice just a little bit of cultivation, my mind is
> difficult to rely on.[19]

He is stating that although liberation is hoped for, and we have the inclination to seek enlightenment, through self-reflection we realize that we
are not in possession of the qualities necessary to consummate that intention. Based on this awareness, we then think that perhaps it is possible to
only practice a portion of the Buddhist path. But by reflecting deeply, we
see that the mind is something that cannot really be relied upon.

This pronouncement is indeed somewhat disheartening. For the purpose of transcending our everyday lives and seeking enlightenment, what
else can we rely upon if not our own minds? This thing that I call "myself"
is truly a deluded being, distant from the buddha-realm, and Jōkei is fully
consumed by this realization. The Yogācāra teaching of sentient beings
lacking the nature for liberation that underlies these phrases, "my nature is
not equal to the task" and "my mind can't be relied upon," is pointing to no
one other than ourselves.

Perhaps it is by becoming separated from the buddha-realm like this,
and becoming completely ambivalent about mind and body, that we can
single-mindedly seek the Buddha's warmth. Jōkei has conjectured that it
may be precisely because one lacks the nature for liberation that this "I"
seeks out the empowerment of the buddhas and wishes for liberation. Furthermore, it is the sentient being who lacks the nature for liberation who
can come to the level of sincerely seeking liberation, and one-pointedly
desiring the Buddha's enlightenment. Here Jōkei's thought on the matter
reaches its final conclusion:

> By means of none other than my foolishness, I know my pos-
> session of the Great Vehicle nature.
> If there is not even a state of [two-vehicle] extinction, how
> could I possibly be lacking the [buddha-]nature?[20]

The "nature of the Great Vehicle" refers to the requisite qualities for attaining enlightenment. Although it sounds contradictory, it is only when we are able to truly reflect on our own folly that we are able to know what we possess within our being, the capability of manifesting liberation equal to that of the Buddha.

We should read this passage knowing that it was at precisely the moment of writing that Jōkei felt released from his feelings of deep depression engendered by the conviction of a lack of buddha-nature as taught by his own Yogācāra school, and that he was able to take a great leap forward toward enlightenment. Hence, we can say that it was precisely the depth of his awareness of himself as a sentient being lacking buddha-nature that made him take his first step *into* the buddha-nature. His arrival to this critical juncture was based on nothing other than his single-minded, penetrating self-examination. And this self-examination was greatly advanced and deepened by his awareness of the composition of the mind and its various psychological functions, as articulated by the Yogācāras.

THE DEVELOPMENT OF THE INTRINSIC UNCONTAMINATED SEEDS

The doctrine of the five natures can only be properly understood in the context of a profound self-examination. If we simply accept the five natures as some sort of doctrinal classification, its deep religious significance is utterly lost. Yogācāra opponents in the Tiantai school evaluated this doctrine as "expedient great vehicle" in some sense, a classification that originates within derogatory intention.

Criticism of others is something to always be restrained, or even better, not done at all. If we who are deeply attached to our selves, and who are under the sway of negative mental factors such as conceit and envy, compare ourselves with others and criticize them while abiding in this condition, we cannot but end up doing nothing but praising ourselves, and either slandering others or envying them.

Thus, the warning against "praising oneself and disparaging others" is a standard injunction in Buddhism. It is specifically proscribed in such texts as the *Bodhisattva Precepts*.[21] But it is not simply the case that we should avoid praising ourselves and disparaging others. What is really implied by this idea is the vital importance of one's continued deepening of one's practice of self-examination.

If I reflect on myself sincerely, isn't it nothing but an afflicted "I" that is coming and going, no matter what—nothing but the same deluded me? And isn't it that this "I" is seeking the mind of liberation, the true enlightenment that lacks deceit and falsehood? At this point, the matter of whether "I" am actually in personal possession of the basic qualities for becoming a buddha is not really especially important. The only thing that matters is that I truly want to seek the state of enlightenment. The mode of this seeking is one of utterly pure single-mindedness. In seeking something like enlightenment, which lacks deceit and falsity, why should we be lacking the prerequisite nature? Jōkei explains: "By none other than my foolishness, I know my possession of the great vehicle nature: If there is not even a state of [two-vehicle] extinction, how could I possibly be lacking the [buddha-]nature?" This great moment of conviction is a point at which one reaches the limits of human conception. We realize that we possess the buddha-nature, and naturally come to the clear conviction that if even I am endowed with the buddha-nature, it should naturally follow that all persons must be endowed with the buddha-nature.

To express the notion that all sentient beings possess the buddha-nature in Yogācāra technical language, we would say that all living beings are endowed with inherent uncontaminated seeds of bodhisattvahood in the latent regions of their consciousnesses. However, we must remember that the storage of innate seeds in the *ālaya-vijñāna* is unconfirmed. Jōkei's personal assertion notwithstanding, the existence or non-existence of the buddha-nature, and the existence or non-existence of the innate uncontaminated seeds of the bodhisattva is something fundamentally unknowable to us. The only one who is able to know this is the Buddha, the only one who has overcome them himself.

We understand that we need to single-mindedly strive toward enlightenment, and practice the Buddha's teachings in our daily lives. While all beings are endowed with this so-called buddha-nature, they are not yet perfected buddhas. If this potentiality to become buddha is not limitlessly developed, it is a terrible waste. A person may be equipped with the inherent uncontaminated seeds of bodhisattvahood, but if he fails to develop, manifestly activate, and amplify these uncontaminated seeds, then realistically speaking, it is the same as if these innate uncontaminated seeds did not exist at all. Yogācāra Buddhism challenges us to develop the potential we are naturally endowed with.

The ability to manifest liberation equal to that of the buddha is an extremely subtle quality, so we should not make light judgments regarding its existence or non-existence. The matter of whether or not we are endowed with qualities within ourselves that will allow us to overcome various obstacles and arrive at enlightenment is something of great interest to us. However, if we look closely at this same self who is concerned about the possession or non-possession of the buddha-nature, and we take the position that there is no buddha-nature, we will be unable to manifest complete liberation. Despite the practice of a Buddhist lifestyle, we will end up in a condition where it is difficult not to feel that our efforts have been in vain. One who is operating under this kind of notion is certainly not attempting to follow the Buddhist path, and can even be seen as "lacking the predisposition for buddhahood."

Jōkei, disgusted with his own delusion, no longer had room in his mind for worrying about the presence, or lack, of the buddha-nature. Whether or not one has the potential to reach the state of the Buddha, this "I" desires the Buddha's peace of mind. Of course, if within myself "I" lack the buddha-nature, "I" cannot attain enlightenment. But even if I can't attain it, I would like to move a single step, or even a half-step, toward the buddha-realm. Jōkei, who deeply respected this kind of determination, understood this to be nothing but precisely the Mahāyāna nature as it should be. Within that determination, one must attempt to tread the Buddhist path, and persist in it. There, leaving aside the matter of the possession of innate uncontaminated seeds, a wonderful opportunity presents itself to gradually turn that so-called concealed nature into something powerful.

In response to the question of what happens to a person who lacks the uncontaminated seeds of the bodhisattvahood (not to mention the seeds for *pratyekabuddha*-hood, or *śrāvaka*-hood), Yogācāra Buddhism teaches that the practice of a Buddhist lifestyle will still bring great benefit at a level appropriate to the character of the individual. This means that there will be an enhancement for the individual in his place within the community, as well as an improvement in one's insight based on the calming effect that comes to body and mind. When teaching the ten precepts[22] to the people, the Venerable Jiun (Onkō; 1718–1804) characterized the ten precepts as "the way to become a human being." This should be a maxim in our daily lives.

Chapter Ten: The Distance to Buddhahood

WHAT ORDINARY PEOPLE COGNIZE AND WHAT BUDDHAS COGNIZE

Human beings, along with all the things in their environment, are born, extinguished, and changing in every single moment. There is not a single thing that is invariable and substantial. We are told that when the Buddha guided deluded people to the world of enlightenment, that this is the kind of teaching he offered. Buddhist teachings assert that if one can completely internalize these two points, one will achieve a considerable level of mental equanimity.

To restate the truth taught by Śākyamuni, all things are brought into existence based on a wide range of causes and conditions. All things (all dharmas), whether they be psychic or material phenomena, occur because various elements harmonize temporarily in specific conditions. Not being established for more than an instant, they absolutely do not exist as fixed, unchanging substances. Therefore, once the provisional combination disintegrates, all phenomena disappear at once. In this way, all dharmas are in a continual state of flux.

In Yogācāra, this manner of occurrence is called the *dependently arisen nature (paratantra-svabhāva)*, meaning that things only exist by virtue of their relationships with other things. All things in this world exist only through this dependently arisen nature. Thus our eight consciousnesses and all of our various mental functions exist like this, and most importantly cognition itself has this dependently arisen character. Nonetheless, we grasp to all cognitive objects, assume them to be substantial, and attach firmly to them. This mental function, which occurs in the sixth and seventh consciousnesses where one understands all dharmas to exist substantially, is called the *nature of attachment to that which is pervasively discriminated (parikalpita-svabhāva)*. We apprehend those things that have a dependently arisen nature by covering them with the net of attachment. Since we understand the things that are actually in a constant state of flux as having a fixed appearance, the things that are cognized by we ordinary persons are said to be *false deceptions*. Our painful lives are rigidly established on the basis of this false cognition, and once formed, are difficult to change.

All things are comprised as nothing but the temporary combinations of a multitude of conditions, which in their process of going from formation to extinction are in a continual state of change. In order for this character of existence to be personally witnessed, one must cease in being trapped by pervasive conceptual reification of things that are actually dependently arisen. Yogācāra Buddhism teaches that when one becomes separated from this habit of mistaken attachment, and correctly sees oneself and all the things that surround oneself from the perspective of their dependently arisen nature, the original mode of existence of each thing appears magnificently before us. This is precisely the content of the Buddha's cognition, and this pure cognition of the dependently arisen nature is expressed by the technical term *perfectly realized true nature (parinispanna-svabhāva)*.

These three modes of cognition—the nature of attachment to that which is pervasively discriminated, the dependently arisen nature, and the perfectly realized true nature—are known as the *three natures*.

An analogy has been used for centuries to describe the three natures. A person walking on a path during the night sees a discarded rope, and misconstrues it to be a snake, and is thus frightened. However, with another hard look, carefully scrutinizing the "snake," it becomes clear that it was merely a rope. The rope comes to be known as a rope. As the person considers this further, he becomes aware that there is actually no substance of a rope, but that it is a composite made up of numerous strands of hemp, and is only provisionally labeled as a rope.

This is called the analogy of the snake, rope, and hemp. The awareness of the hemp is equivalent to the perfectly realized true nature; the awareness that the rope is composed of the various causes and conditions of the hemp shows the dependently arisen nature. And the mistaken understanding of the rope to be a snake represents the nature of attachment to that which is pervasively discriminated. This *three natures doctrine* is one of the most important in Yogācāra Buddhism.

Here, we have given nothing but the barest introduction to the teaching of the three natures, but hopefully the path that is to be advanced upon has been sufficiently described. Its orientation leads toward extracting oneself from the cognition done by ordinary people through attachment to that which is pervasively discriminated, and to strive for the cognition through the viewpoint of the Buddha's perfectly realized true nature.

What exactly might be this path be that leads from the level of the ordinary person to that of the Buddha? What could be of more concern to us than this? Let's now take a look at some interpretations of the nature and content of the path that leads to liberation.

The Sudden Teaching and the Gradual Teaching

Let us once again recall the words of Jōkei: "By none other than my foolishness, I know my possession of the great vehicle nature." Through a penetrating self-examination, Jōkei became aware of his delusion, while clearly realizing a self that sought honestly for the Buddha's empowerment. And to the extent that he held on to the single-minded feeling of intention toward enlightenment, try as he might to be a sentient being lacking the nature for liberation, he strongly felt within himself the quality of a direct connection to the Buddha, the bodhisattva nature.

With the turns in the mind of this great master of Yogācāra, we find that it is exactly in the realization of the hopelessness of our own self-delusion, the deep sense of how we are truly sentient beings lacking the nature for buddhahood, that the first step toward buddha-nature is taken. In other words, it is precisely within the coming to awareness of one's own delusion that the great decision is formed to seek enlightenment, despite obstructions. And, it seems that we can understand that this decision, the prompting of the so-called *arousal of intention* (for enlightenment), means that it is here that the substantial start toward the buddha-realm can be identified.

By confronting our true feelings in this early period of our Buddhist practice, it will naturally follow that we will make any efforts possible to bring
about the manifestation of the Buddha's liberation as soon as possible.

Leaving aside our own feelings on the topic for a moment, Buddhist
notions regarding the process of liberation can be generally divided into the
approaches of the *sudden teaching* and the *gradual teaching*. The sudden
teaching is the idea that liberation equal to the buddhas can be attained
rapidly. This is represented in such statements by adherents of the sudden
position such as "accomplishing buddhahood in this body." On the other
hand, the gradual teaching takes the position that our tenacious attachments to self and dharmas are things that cannot be instantly severed, and
can only be gradually eliminated by sustained exertion, and therefore the
accomplishment of buddhahood is something that requires training over
a vast period of time.

Here Yogācāra Buddhism takes the gradualist position.

No doubt, if presented with a choice between these two approaches, the
majority of people are likely to express a preference for the sudden teaching. However, those of us who are inclined toward rapid attainment of
buddhahood should first consider one point. A rapid progression can only
be fulfilled if one begins on a strong foundation of the accumulation of
honest effort. The gradual teaching is an approach that clearly prioritizes
the honest accumulation of one's efforts, the cultivation of the six
*pāramitā*s and practice of the four methods of winning people over, treading on the way of being human. Based on this daily honest accumulation
of goodness, enlightenment cannot but naturally spring up from within
oneself. The rapid attainment of buddhahood can be considered as an end
result of this long and continuous accumulation.

It is, in fact, not so easy to maintain a perfect Buddhist lifestyle in our
normal daily life. If we reflect on our life as one in which we should be
aiming for enlightenment, it is something in which we continually move
toward, and then retreat, from our goal. At such a time, we will come to an
understanding of the meaning of the gradual teaching that places emphasis on the honest accumulation of goodness.

In the seminal Yogācāra text entitled *Mahāyāna-saṃgrāha,* the great
Indian master of Yogācāra doctrine, Asaṅga (fifth century) wrote: "the

mastery over vows is accomplished by completing the transcendent practice of zeal." Zeal involves facing one's goal, steadily striving without distraction, proceeding toward its accomplishment without any lapse whatsoever. But while this is an ideal lifestyle, it is not so easy to put it into practice. The Buddhist lifestyle is something that can only be accomplished through the accumulation of one's efforts, one day at a time.

ACCOMPLISHMENT OF BUDDHAHOOD IN THREE EONS AND THE FIVE STAGES OF YOGĀCĀRA CULTIVATION

Yogācāra Buddhists deeply considered all facets of the mind, and made an effort to clarify its actual composition and workings. From their perspective, it is certain that neither our attachment to self nor attachment to dharmas can be easily severed. Rather, they can only be eliminated gradually over a long period of steady practice. The course in which we awaken our mind and tread the path of the bodhisattva, and finally fully attain liberation, is definitely something that is neither short, smooth, nor sudden.

So exactly how long *is* this "long period of steady practice"? For we ordinary people who think continuously of buddhahood, but are on the other hand rather lazy, this is something to be very anxious about.

Yogācāra commonly expresses the notion of a very long time with the term *three great asaṃkhya kalpas* or *three [great] kalpas and one hundred kalpas. Asaṃkhya* is a Sanskrit term that means "incalculable" or "innumerable" and *kalpa* is an Indian concept that indicates a vast period of time, similar to the English *eon*. This terminology indicates that the path to attainment of buddhahood taught by Yogācāra Buddhism is something that definitely cannot be accomplished in a short period of time, but rather requires an incalculably long time to complete. In order to understand this incalculably long period of time, the two metaphors of the "rock-dusting kalpa" and the "mustard-seed kalpa" have been employed since ancient times.

In the metaphor of the rock-dusting kalpa, the feathery robe of an angel brushes across a great stone eight hundred miles in breadth once every hundred years. The thinness and lightness of the feathery robe of the angel can be thought of as something like the thin cloth used for a woman's blouse. The time required to finally wear down the megalith by lightly brushing it with this kind of robe gives the sense of one great *asaṃkhya* kalpa. Three times this amount is called three great *asaṃkhya* kalpas.

In the metaphor of the mustard seed, tiny mustard seeds are dropped into the courtyard of a castle that is eight hundred miles across, one seed every hundred years. The time it takes to fill the castle courtyard via this process is called a mustard-seed kalpa. Whether it be the metaphor of the rock-dusting kalpa or the mustard-seed kalpa, what is being referred to is nothing short of an eternity. In other words, what the Yogācāras are saying is that without carrying out religious cultivation for an incredibly long time, it is impossible to free ourselves from our bonds and attain enlightenment. Therefore, in opposition to the theory that one can suddenly manifest the realization of the Buddha, they instead advocate the attainment of buddhahood in the course of three *asaṃkhya* kalpas.

The term, *three asaṃkhya kalpas plus one hundred kalpas* does not mean that one hundred additional kalpas are required in addition to the three great *asaṃkhya* kalpas. The one hundred kalpas are to be understood as being included within the three *asaṃkhya* kalpas.

It is believed that the true bodhisattva, who in his practice of the six *pāramitā*s and so forth has nearly completed the buddha-path, will carry out the wholesome karmic activities that engender the manifestation of the bodily features that are unique to the buddhas only during his final hundred kalpas. The bodily features that will appear on him are known as the excellent thirty-two major characteristics and eighty minor characteristics that are found on the Buddha's body. Based on these marks, if a true buddha is present, he can be readily identified. For instance, as the *Sūtra of the Account of Travels*[23] says: "Replete with the major and minor characteristics, he is like the moon among the stars." This means that the major and minor characteristics are gradually developed over the long course of one hundred kalpas. This is the meaning of *three [great] kalpas and one hundred kalpas*.

While Buddhism is known for its focus on developing the mind, it is also a typically Buddhist approach to see the body and mind not as two separate entities, but as a unity. By training through an eternity, we will gradually sever various afflictions. Accordingly, the long and great Buddha-path of three incalculably long kalpas can be divided into a number of stages of gradual improvement.

In Yogācāra Buddhism, these stages are understood to be the five stages of preparation, application, insight, cultivation, and final, and are thus named the *five stages of the Yogācāra path of cultivation*. Among these, the first four stages are those in which one practices with the aim of becoming a buddha. They serve as the causes of buddhahood, and are collectively called the *causal stages*. On the other hand, the final stage is where the bodhisattva becomes Buddha based on this development. Because becoming Buddha is a result of training, it is called the *buddha-result*. The buddha-result is understood as containing both bodhi and nirvāṇa, and thus it is thought to be something so marvelous that it exceeds the possibilities of linguistic expression. The fact that the true bodhisattva, through cultivation in three great kalpas and one hundred kalpas, attains the state of liberation equal to that of the buddhas has been known since ancient times as the *realization of the marvelous result of bodhi and nirvāṇa*.

In the first stage of preparation, one engages in all kinds of wholesome practices, and sets one's sights on buddhahood. Of course, the arousal of the intention to attain enlightenment occupies an important place in this first step. Based on a deep belief and understanding the Yogācāra view, clearly seeking for buddhahood, and a steady determination to actualize *bodhi* and nirvāṇa, we can truly make a start at the Buddha-path of three *asaṃkhya* kalpas. The ability to be able to continually tread on the Buddha-path is dependent on such a consistent arousal of intention.

The personal realization of all things being nothing but the transformations of consciousness begins to take place in the third stage of insight, but in order to reach to that level, it is necessary to step up to the level of directly cultivating through the application of effort, the stage of application.

Our various mental disturbances serve as major obstacles in the attainment of buddhahood, and these are divided into the two general types of afflictive hindrances and cognitive hindrances, and are further distinguished into the two categories of those *arisen by discrimination* and those that are *innately arisen*. *Innately arisen* refers to mental disturbances in the categories of the two hindrances which are inborn. In contrast to these, *arisen by discrimination* refers to the mental disturbances in the categories of the two kinds of hindrances that are taken on subsequent to our birth in this world. As one might expect, inborn afflictions are much harder to remove than those that are produced by discrimination.

Within these mental disturbances, at the stage of preparation and the stage of application of practices, only the manifest activity of the discriminatively arisen afflictive and cognitive hindrances is quelled. Quelling their manifest activity means that the arousal of afflictive and cognitive hindrances from their seeds is suppressed, but the seeds of the afflictive and cognitive hindrances themselves are not eliminated.

In the third stage, the stage of insight, one eliminates the seeds of the discriminatively arisen afflictive and cognitive hindrances, giving rise to uncontaminated wisdom, and as a result gains insight into the principle of the world being nothing but the mere transformations of consciousness.

Once one has fully attained the insight into the principle that all things are merely the transformations of our cognitive processes, one renews efforts at spiritual practice based on this insight in the next stage, the fourth stage of cultivation. In this stage, the manifest activity of the inborn afflictive hindrances and cognitive hindrances is quelled, and, moreover, their seeds are gradually eliminated. The Yogācāras break this stage down into ten levels wherein, up to the seventh level, the practitioner still needs to apply conscious effort to the application of meditative practices. But from the eighth level onward, applied effort is no longer needed, and one practices the buddha-path effortlessly.

The true bodhisattva, in the causal stages from the stage of preparation up to the stage of cultivation, first works at quelling the manifest activity of the afflictions, then removes their seeds, and finally dispels the remaining karmic impressions and dispositions of afflicted mental activity that have adhered within his person. The course of practice as defined in terms of the elimination of afflictions through these causal stages is called *quelling, eliminating, and dispelling.* Once all mental disturbances have been completely quelled, eliminated, and shaken off, one reaches to the fifth and final stage.

The final stage is the stage of completion of the long buddha-path after three *asaṃkhya* kalpas. Here, the bodhisattva realizes the marvelous fruits of bodhi and nirvāṇa, and finally becomes a buddha. As explained earlier, nirvāṇa is a state of equanimity of the mind and body, manifested as a result of the full removal of all afflictive hindrances. Bodhi is the uncontaminated wisdom that knows things exactly as they are, which is attained by the elimination of the cognitive hindrances. This wisdom that apprehends things exactly as they are is the standard cognitive function of the buddhas. This means that none other than our eight consciousnesses that are the subject of our cognitive processes are, at the new dawn after three *asaṃkhya* kalpas of practice, qualitatively transformed. This is called *the wisdom attained as the transformation of the consciousnesses*.

In this, the *ālaya-vijñāna* is recreated, becoming the *perfect mirror cognition*. The *manas* is recreated, becoming the *cognition of essential equality*. The thinking consciousness is recreated, becoming the *cognition of unerring observation*. And the prior five consciousnesses are recreated, becoming the *cognitions with unrestricted activity*. These four types of cognitive activity form the content of bodhi.

We can now begin to pay some special attention to the *cognition of essential equality*. We know that the *manas* is a subconscious form of mind which misconstrues the continuing-as-a-single-kind *ālaya-vijñāna* to be a real self, attaching firmly to it. Arriving to the final stage, the selfish latent mind becomes an unsullied true cognition that sees self and other equally without distinction. There is an incredible distance between my selfishness and Buddha's compassion, a distance that is a Buddha-path of three *asaṃkhya* kalpas—in other words, an eternity. Considering this eternal striving, we may experience the tendency to take it in a leisurely manner. We are used to making sure that our lives are filled with speed and convenience. We create a framework in which we take delight in simplicity and ease, valuing shortcuts and quick completions. Given this kind of quick-results oriented framework that we have created in our daily lives, the Buddha-path of three *asaṃkhya* kalpas obviously cannot be accommodated.

However, coming to understand the extent of our folly, we realize the need to dismantle all the frameworks used up to now in the handling of our daily lives. Hidden roughly underneath the feeling that seeks for convenience is a cheap frame of mind that seeks to avoid obstacles. The more things that can be avoided, the better. To try to hold on to this approach, and at the same time seeking liberation in the quelling, elimination, and dispelling of the afflictions, seems to be extremely selfish, and an inappropriate attitude for traversing along the Buddhist path.

Buddhism tends to apprehend things in terms of very long spans of time. Or, one might say that it exhibits the special characteristic of a tendency not to cut things off in terms of temporal limits. For instance, a good example can be seen in the "declaration of the three refuges," such as "My disciples, extending into the limits of the future, take refuge in the Buddha, take refuge in the dharma, and take refuge in the *sangha*." This is an expression of taking refuge in the three treasures of Buddha, dharma, *sangha*, going beyond the limits of the future. "Limits of the future" of course refers to something that can never be exhausted, and thus what is basically implied is an eternity. Therefore, if we paraphrase it, it means "no matter where," "no matter when," etc. We who are the disciples of the Buddha will take refuge in the Buddha, take refuge in his dharma, and take refuge in the *sangha* for as long as is necessary, placing no limits. This is the meaning of the "declaration of the three refuges." Thus, "taking refuge" is something initially taken up with a view extending into the eternal future, in other words, something boundless, and, in that sense, the notion of "no matter how far" has very important implications.

This means that we if we would become awakened to our own folly, aim ourselves toward enlightenment, and become determined to henceforth turn our life into a real Buddhist life, we must not shrink from the vast time of the three *asaṃkhya* kalpas. Rather, we must resolutely accept the perspective of "no matter how long it takes." And, we must know that within this incredibly long Buddhist life that extends to "no matter how long it takes," the standard fare of the ordinary person's life with its love of ready usability, cheapness, shortcuts, and hasty sloppiness will not be countenanced. We should know that only the continued honest accumulation of goodness will push us up into the buddha-realm. And this is precisely the content of the first stage taught in Yogācāra, the stage of preparation. In another sense, it is consistently sought throughout the buddha-path in the three *asaṃkhya* kalpas.

The relationship between the five stages and the three *asaṃkhya* kalpas is shown in the table below.

stage of preparation	first *asaṃkhya* kalpa
stage of application	
stage of insight	second *asaṃkhya* kalpa
stage of cultivation (levels one to seven)	
stage of cultivation (levels eight to ten)	third *asaṃkhya* kalpa
final stage	

RETROGRESSION AND TRAINING

The long Yogācāra path of cultivation begins with the stage of preparation. At this point, the "I" has come to profoundly understand its own folly and yearns strongly for the buddha-realm, eventually cultivating a firm resolution to reach to the buddha-realm despite obstacles. This firm resolution to continue treading the Buddhist path no matter what may occur, entrusting one's entire self in such a resolution without reservation, is expressed with the Buddhist term *firm abiding in the arousal of the intention*. This abiding in the arousal of the intention, which is anything but a careless or perfunctory decision, is precisely the point of departure for the stage of preparation.

Next, the true bodhisattva carries out various wholesome activities, honestly accumulating the necessary provisions for the seeking of the buddha-realm. This stage is considered the most important stage in that if such provisions have not been fully accumulated, the bodhisattva will be unable to proceed to the second stage, the stage of application of practices. The wholesome practices that are to be carried out in this stage include the six *pāramitā*s and four methods of winning people over, and those who are focused on the bodhisattva path should implement them in their daily lives.

The matter of donation has already been addressed to some extent in the context of the three rings of purity (cf. chapter 6, "The Deep Self Absorbed in Selfishness," the section entitled "The Second Subjective Transformation: The *Manas*," and chapter 9, "Who Am I?" the section entitled "Sentient Beings Lacking the Nature for Buddhahood"). Therefore, I will refrain from repeating that here. But the significance of donation that is taught in Buddhism, wherein if requested, one should even offer up one's own life, cannot but profoundly move us. The buddha-realm that cannot be reached unless this donation is carried out perfectly might be seen as something too overwhelming, even for the person focused on bodhisattvahood with unshakably firm determination. Faced with this buddha-realm of such vast infinitude, one is bewildered, hesitates, and loses confidence in the worth of continuing to endeavor in the Buddhist lifestyle. It is said that such vacillation is often seen in Buddhist practice at the first stage of preparation. This is called *retrogression* (or *backsliding*). While taking buddhahood as one's goal, instead of leaping forward, one retreats and vacillates. The stage of preparation of the first title of the Yogācāra path of cultivation is not a stage of smooth progress, but is characterized by meandering and vicissitudes.

In what ways were the early founders of Buddhist faced with situations of retrogression like this? One of the most beneficial examples centers on the greatest of Śākyamuni's disciples, Śāriputra.

There is a tradition (derived from the *Mahā-prajñāpāramitā-śastra*) that says that although Śāriputra is usually known as someone who attained enlightenment as a *śrāvaka,* he was originally not a *śrāvaka,* but a person practicing the bodhisattva path aimed at buddhahood. According to this story, Śāriputra reverted to the *śrāvaka* path because he lapsed in his long-maintained practice of donation. A certain Brahman (a priest who administers the ancient ritual sacrifice) came to Śāriputra, begging for his eye. Śāriputra responded to him by saying, "Since an eyeball alone will be of no use, allow me to offer my whole body to you." However, the Brahman, obstinately demanding Śāriputra's eyeball, said: "If you are genuinely practicing donation, you should simply give me your eye, as I requested." Indeed, in the practice of donation, one is only supposed to give what is begged for. So, Śāriputra plucked out one of his eyeballs, and handed it over to the eye-begging Brahman.

What happened next is rather shocking. The Brahman, smelling the eye that Śāriputra offered to him, blurted out, "Pew! It stinks!" He threw the eyeball on the ground, and crushed it under his foot. He had begged for something that he had not really needed, simply to test Śāriputra's practice of donation. Śāriputra, watching this with his remaining eye, furiously thought, "What a sick thing to do!" Then he thought, "Such a wicked person is indeed difficult to save. Even if he follows the Buddhist path and cultivates his entire being, he will not so quickly attain liberation from the deluded realm of birth and death." Reassessing his practice in the context of this experience, he backed off from the bodhisattva path that is tread on the basis of donation, and turned to the path of the śrāvaka.

Śāriputra often delivered sermons in the place of Śākyamuni, and even later became known as the "disciple who re-turned the wheel of the dharma." He is sometimes described by likening Buddha to a tree, and Śāriputra to the flowers that adorn it. If it was a very difficult matter to carry out donation perfectly for such a practitioner as excellent as Śāriputra, how much more difficult it must be for we ordinary unenlightened people?

The cases of retrogression are classified into three types.

The first involves the practitioner becoming profoundly aware of the vastness and depth of the content of the enlightenment realized by the buddhas, and feeling that one's own capacity will be wholly insignificant for the task. This is called *wavering due to a sense of vastness.*

The second is the case where the practitioner, upon attempting the transcendent practice of donation, the six *pāramitā*s, and the whole gamut of the great vehicle path, becomes profoundly aware of the difficulty of carrying out such practices to completion, and thus gives rise to thoughts of abandonment of the path. This is called *wavering due to a sense of the difficulty of the number of practices.*

The third is the case in which the practitioner realizes that it is extremely difficult to attain the realization of the Buddha, and begins to develop a pessimistic view, which leads to retrogression. This is called *wavering due to awareness of the difficulty of attaining the Buddha's realization.*

Although one may take strong first steps with a firm abiding in the arousal of the intention for enlightenment, the person aiming for bodhisattvahood may easily feel overwhelmed, and develop a pessimistic attitude concerning one's own nature and capacity. Despite our initial intentions, it is not easy to remain immovably focused on the bodhisattva ideal.

There is a line from the *Mahāprajñāpāramitā-śāstra* that says:

The bodhisattva, for the duration of one hundred thousand kalpas, does not give rise to anger when reviled, and does not give rise to joy when praised.

The one who is not at all moved by any kind of praise or abuse is a true bodhisattva, because the bodhisattva's mind and body are single-mindedly focused on the attainment of enlightenment. We ordinary people spend much of our daily life being praised by others or being slandered by them, all the while bouncing up and down between elation and gloom. This is because we are lacking in single-minded attention to our target. But by keeping the bodhisattva path in the foremost of our mind, we will not be shaken by any kind of evaluation.

Even if the three kinds retrogression of wavering due to a sense of vast-ness, wavering due to an awareness of the difficulty of the number of prac-tices, and wavering due to awareness of the difficulty of realizing the Buddha's enlightenment cannot be avoided in the stage of preparation, one should still refuse to give up on the Buddha-path. Concerning these three kinds of retrogression, Yogācāra says:

Polishing their minds, the courageous do not waver.

This phrase is repeated several times in the *Cheng weishi lun*.[24] It provides us with encouragement in our moments of hesitation. We are attempting to reach the buddha-realm, the actualization of a Buddhist lifestyle. Our immediate target should be nothing other than learning how to abide firmly in the arousal of the intention for enlightenment, but we are aware that the path to this state is fraught with the influence of retrogression in the form of pessimistic dispositions. At such a time, we can find considerable encour-agement in the phrase "in polishing their minds, the courageous do not waver." We should receive this clearly and purely, allowing it to resonate deeply within our being, providing strength for our minds that fall so eas-ily into retrogression. We come to fully realize the great opportunity being made available for steady and certain advancement along the Buddha-path.

Conclusion: Yogācāra Today

AWAKENING TO THE TRUE NATURE OF OTHER-DEPENDENCY

Over the course of ten chapters, we have conducted an overview of the composition and function of our minds, broadly learning about the mental mechanism as is explained in Yogācāra Buddhism. In doing so, we have continually placed emphasis on the aspect of the application of Yogācāra in one's daily life. But beyond the mere instruction in doctrine, or explication of technical terminology, we have continuously tried to demonstrate how we can bring benefit to our daily lives using these principles.

In considering our mind as explained by Yogācāra teachings, we may begin to question the reality of self-cognition as a person living everyday life. We are forced to realize that it is not "reality" at all—rather it seems to be far removed from anything that could be considered "real."

But to this end, Yogācāra lays special stress on the fact that the content of our cognition arises in dependence upon the *ālaya-vijñāna,* after which it is subject to three distinguishable layers of alteration. It is possible for us to remain quite distantly removed from the Buddhist ideals of "knowing ourselves as we really are," or "perceiving those things that surround us as they really are." Indeed, we can live a mere virtual reality.

This falsely cognized world was identified above as the *nature of attachment to that which is pervasively discriminated* in the three natures doctrine. All things, including the self, come to be as a result of the provisional harmonization of various factors under a certain set of conditions. And although they appear to exist in a stable permanence, they are in fact continually changing. Although the dependently arisen and ceaselessly changing phenomenal world that we inhabit is originally of the *dependently arisen nature,* we inadvertently take it to be something substantial. Additionally, we ceaselessly crave the things we find to be suitable, are disgusted with the things we find to be unsuitable, and finally, we attach deeply to these feelings of revulsion. This is the world of nature of attachment to that which is pervasively discriminated, the state in which we are actually living.

Those of us who have learned something about the real state of our cognition and attachment are not satisfied to simply follow one or two minor practices, but instead wish for the full removal of false attachment to that which is pervasively discriminated. We can only then awaken to the other-dependent nature of these momentary phenomena produced according to the coalescence of various conditions, which continue in the flux of prior extinction and subsequent arising.

Though the essence of this other-dependency is none other than the *perfectly true nature,* it is taught in Buddhism that the perfectly real world is disclosed by the profound awareness of the empty character of all things. What is of crucial importance is to firmly acquire the habit of remaining aware that all things, including oneself, are not permanent substances, but that they are in a continuous state of flux.

At the beginning, this kind of practice is not so simple. But in cultivating the awareness that we now have, we realize that our present mode of cognition somehow seems to be different from "truth" or "reality," and from that, we need to further deepen our self-examination. If we carry on with this honest effort, the extremely tenacious veil of attachment to that which is pervasively discriminated should be gradually removed, just like the peeling off of a thin skin.

YOGĀCĀRA AND THE LIFE SCIENCES

In recent years, the life sciences have progressed rapidly, and those things that were heretofore considered to be under the domain of God alone have been revealed and accounted for one after another. We are constantly being amazed by the complex scientific world around us. But this scientific world is not at all incompatible with Buddhism. On the contrary, both agree with the basic position that human beings do not possess some kind of supremacy or special honor, but instead have the fundamental character of simply being one kind of being dwelling in the midst of nature.

With current research in genetics and the charting of the full human genome, there has been an increased tendency to try to engage these concepts with such Yogācāra notions as seeds, or the *ālaya-vijñāna*. Questions have been posed as to whether it is possible to explain the genome from the perspective of the *ālaya-vijñāna,* or whether *genes* and *seeds* can be said to be the same thing.

At present, such questions have still not gone beyond the level of idle talk. But for Buddhists who live in society and who have a keen interest in the rapid developments of life science, I think that this sort of dialogue is important. However, there are Buddhists who have gone so far as to flatly claim from the Yogācāra perspective that seeds are genes. This is no doubt an apologetic stance that takes the Yogācāra doctrine as something excellent that provides an explanation of state-of-the-art scientific findings and should be thus valued. But this should not be considered the case.

If seeds were indeed equivalent to genes, the *ālaya-vijñāna* would be considered the entire genome, as it is the consciousness containing all seeds. Certainly, it is said that the deep mind of the *ālaya-vijñāna* takes as its three cognitive objects the *seeds, body with faculties,* and *natural world,* appropriating these. Among these, the *body with faculties* is the physical body, and therefore it is clearly understood that the *ālaya-vijñāna* is deeply bound to the body. While many say that the deep mind of the *ālaya-vijñāna* is a mind unlimited in its closeness of connections to the body, even without these claims it must be admitted that this deep mind is a mental basis that has a certain relationship with the body.

Yogācāra Buddhism argues that all causes are to be found within "transformations of consciousness," and phenomena are reduced to being "mental factors." As long as our understanding of Yogācāra is based on this, seeds and human genetics are beyond comparison. Human genes are transmitted from parents to their children, and fundamentally consist of matter containing manipulative potentiality. Physical genes cannot be equated with the mental-energy seeds that impregnate our actions into the deep mind of the store consciousness.

As we have seen repeatedly, our actions are never finished or complete. The energy accompanying the wholesomeness or unwholesomeness of the act is perfumed into the *ālaya-vijñāna,* and seeds impregnated into the depths of the mind are, no matter how inconvenient for the present self, not something that can be simply manipulated. Exactly because of this, we realize that the seeds create the basis for our actions, permeating the depths of our minds. They are wholly different from the human genetic code.

To a Buddhist, life is not started based only upon the joining of the sperm and ovum. The *life-binding consciousness* is necessary in the joining of the essences of the mother and father, and without this, it is understood that there can be no life. This life-binding consciousness is none other than the *ālaya-vijñāna.*

According to the theory of transmigration, we have many prior lives, and it is only because we were unable to let go of our attachment to life in our most recent past life that, at the moment of death, our *ālaya-vijñāna* becomes the life-binding consciousness, and detaching itself, depends upon the next appropriate combination of the two drops of red and white. This constitutes the moment of death as understood in Buddhism.

Following this line of thought, the external form of the body may be inherited from the sperm and egg of the parents. But the contents of this body, the seeds that are the cause of manifest activities, are something that has been inherited from one's past lives as far back as they extend. Again we can refute the claim that the genes passed down from parent to child are the same as the seeds of Yogācāra. We are confronted with the distinction made in seed theory, between *intrinsic* and *newly perfumed,* as well as the distinction between seeds that are *uncontaminated* and *contaminated.* It's safe to assume that no one will argue that genes can be distinguished into uncontaminated and contaminated groups.

Buddhists who live in ages henceforth will continue to debate advanced findings made by researchers in the life sciences. But if we make these correspondences based on a superficially felt sense of similarity, we will accomplish nothing but the invitation of useless confusion. We should instead hold firm to the Yogācāra position that reduces all things to mental factors, examine the differences closely, and then establish any correspondences to be made based on that.

CONSCIOUS ACTIVITY AND THE PRESENT AGE

Yogācāra Buddhism is a teaching that seeks to fathom the origin of all things in the deep, unconscious mind called the *ālaya-vijñāna*—the dependent arising of the *ālaya-vijñāna*. However, at the same time, our consciously aware activity impregnates the depths of that mind with new seeds, and thus the question of conscious activity is crucial in Yogācāra. To some extent, it is one of our only options for advancing toward enlightenment. As the thinking consciousness is subjected to the powerful influences of the manas, though there may be a conscious intention within the thinking consciousness to attain enlightenment, this is inevitably skewed by the self-centeredness and ego attachment of the manas. But we are helpless, and can only try to activate the powerful self awareness and intentionality of our thinking consciousness.

Emphasizing this point, the Yogācāras say:

Seeds produce manifest activity; manifest activity perfumes seeds; three processes follow each other in sequence with cause and effect occurring simultaneously.

This is the mechanism of our minds. That which produces our manifest activities are the seeds in the *ālaya-vijñāna* (seeds generating manifest activity), while at the same time, the energy from those manifest activities is being planted back into the *ālaya-vijñāna* (manifest activity perfuming seeds). The instantaneous alternation between the seeds and manifest activity as the causes and effects of each other is called *simultaneous cause and effect*. And it is within that subtle alteration that our opportunity lies for improvement or degradation. This manifest mental activity that impregnates the subsequently differing seeds into the depths of the mind holds a profound significance, and the function of the thinking consciousness that is involved in this process, no matter how subtle it may be, is something that cannot be overlooked.

Scientific research has shown that we experience roughly 60,000 thoughts passing through our mind each day. What is more interesting, however, is that about 95 percent of these are the same thoughts we had yesterday. One could say that we are carrying out lives in a stagnant way with little change, but if we change the perspective and take notice of the fact that five percent is different from the past, then this accumulation of small acts should be something that carries a deep and fundamental significance. The problem is, however, that the deep significance of each conscious act gradually loses its relevance in the greater context of our society.

Modern society has, in its single-minded pursuit of material resources and convenience, been able to tread the path of economic prosperity, and based upon the recent revolution in information technology, is reaching for an even greater efficiency-prioritized society. Thanks to this, we can be connected to the latest updated information without leaving the comfort of our homes, and as a result, our daily life becomes steadily more convenient.

It is not an exaggeration to say that everything is "upgraded" daily, and that this moment knows no limit. To stay abreast of this advanced age, we must lead life in such as way as to keep focused on keeping up with new developments every day. But does this allow us time to think over what we did a year ago, or even just six months ago? Or, how has the chain of our actions led us to precisely this situation at this point in time? If pressed to clearly articulate these implications, many people would probably be utterly bewildered. As we advance further and further, our actions become trivialized, to the point that our actions seem to be as insignificant as paper fluttering in the breeze.

Our world can be considered a permanent *movement*. The terrific transformation of society, just like the television talk shows, is characterized by an unbroken tedium of empty chatter, continuing without a gasp for fresh air. There is not the slightest space for a moment of stillness. It is nothing but words surging like a flood, with the audience laughing "Ha Ha Ha" and not taking the slightest notice. In the end, there is nothing to show for it. Afterward, a sense of vacancy remains, but cannot be examined in a close and deliberate manner due to the hectic pace of our lives. We move to seek the next moment of horseplay, wandering aimlessly. New information tirelessly surges in.

Within human beings and all the various phenomena created by human beings, the aspects of movement and stillness originally maintain a state of equilibrium. But in the day-to-day survival of our daily life we concentrate on the aspect of movement, and the passing days inevitably become distant. Our individual actions and behavior are regarded as having little significance. The recent remarkable decline in ethics in every place, and at every level of society, has much of its origin in this.

Under these kinds of circumstances, living life under the daily deluge of new information, we eventually push to recover our lost personal time and sense of stillness. But at this point Yogācāra questions the profound significance of human activity. As the effects of our actions are never finished, the energy that carries the wholesome or unwholesome quality of the act is impressed to some extent or another in the depths of the mind, and the remaining energy-as-seeds of the act are impregnated into the ālaya-vijñāna. These qualities are transmitted through all eternity, continuing as latent potentiality within the ālaya-vijñāna. Since this is all happening in a region of mind that is inaccessible to the waking consciousness, no matter how inconvenient the existence of such seeds may turn out to be for the situation of the present self, not the slightest thing can be done about them. Eishun, the learned monk of Kōfukuji Temple whom we have cited previously, composed this deeply impressive verse:

Whatever one experiences, the reliable and incorruptible seeds capture it. (Tamon'in nikki)

Once seeds have been perfumed into the ālaya-vijñāna one can rely on the fact that they will never decay; depending on their being firmly and clearly assimilated, the significance of one's activities is confirmed. With this awareness, one should naturally avoid superficial frivolity, and become conscious of it in others.

This is the driving force behind the mental mechanism of seeds generating manifest activity and manifest activity perfuming seeds that makes the seeds of the first process and the seeds of the third process somewhat different. And, once again, the maintenance of such awareness is clearly our conscious problem.

Since the seeds of this vast amount of accumulated actions and behaviors are planted in the depths of our minds, eventually the ālaya-vijñāna taken as a whole has all of our past actions as its content. In other words, people are nothing other than what they create by their own activities. No matter how dramatically transformed a society in which I must live, my own actions are certainly not something to be regarded as being insignificant. Nay, we may begin to naturally see them as carrying profound meaning.

In this way, in our renewed recognition of the importance of our activities—including the most commonplace and mundane, the study of the mental mechanism understood by Yogācāra Buddhism can play a very effective role.

Afterword

Yōen (1048–1125), who was the thirtieth steward of Kōfukuji as well as the Assistant Head of the Order, was evaluated quite highly by public opinion. For example, in the *Center-Right Record* it says "Among the monks of the North and South, he has no equal." To our regret, it is not clear as to whether any of his writings are extant, but it seems that he was considered to be quite an eminent master of the Yogācāra doctrine in his time. Yōen was also called by the elegant nickname Primary Sound High Priest, which came about due to his fame as a poet. Yōen wrote poetry prolifically, having played an instrumental part in the rise of the medieval world of poetry in the Southern capital, going on to sponsor the Yōen Nara poetry contest. Thus he was a person with deep affinities with art and literature.

So it seems as if he was a person with a talent for poetry, but he was at the same time taken by some onlookers to be someone who did *nothing other* than poetry. In the *Selected Excerpts* is it written that monks who were his close friends came to him to express concerns that too much absorption in poetry could end up becoming a hindrance to his studies of Buddhist doctrine. However, Yōen answered them by saying "This is definitely not the case. Rather, by reading poetry, my mind becomes more and more clear, and through the objects of poetry, I come to better understand the principle of mind-only." Yōen's and his monk friend's appreciation for poetry seem to have been quite different from each other.

The point is not simply to say that this kind of thing happens a lot, but that our daily lives are made up of nothing but these kinds of differences in perspective. Once we give rise to our personal view, we have a tendency to rigidly stick to it. And it is precisely this sort of thing that is the major source of the various obstructions that arise to hinder human relationships that would otherwise be very rich.

At such a time, having ready access to the Yogācāra teachings on the composition and function of the mind can be extremely meaningful. What is most important is that Yogācāra lucidly presents to us the real situation of the mind and its objects, which are more accurately seen as the *subjectively transforming mind* and the *objects that are transformed by our mind's cognition*. Within the continual verification of the self as illuminated by the Yogācāra understanding of the true state of our mind, we have a great opportunity to form a far richer view of things, and of humanity.

Because this book is written for the purpose of trying to place Yogācāra in one's daily life, there has been an attempt to explain matters as simply as possible, and thus many Yogācāra topics that are in fact far more complicated and nuanced have only received the most general of descriptions. For example, in the explanation of the transformation of the consciousnesses into correct cognitions, I explained the four perfected cognitions as all being attained at the level of the final stage. However, to be more precise, the Yogācāra texts say that one begins to partially attain the *marvelous observing cognition* and the *cognition of equality in nature* starting from the first level of the stage of insight, with the *great mirror cognition* and the *cognition with unrestricted activity* being attained only at the final stage. I also did not go into detail explaining technical processes of the subjective transformations, to show exactly how wholesome and unwholesome activities all end up in their fruition as being of indeterminate karmic moral quality. In other words, I decided to omit a lot of standard Yogācāra technical baggage, in the hope of preventing newcomers from getting bogged down in too many details at the beginning.

It might be pointed out that the inclusion of some more commonly-used Yogācāra technical terminology would have been desirable, as this may have aided in the memorization of difficult concepts. But my approach was to avoid, as much as possible, the usage of terminology that I thought would be difficult, trying instead to render these concepts in everyday language. Nonetheless, I still have some concerns as to whether in fact I have ended up making some things more difficult to understand, or if I may have drifted a bit from the original doctrines. I hope that intelligent readers will correct my errors.

However, if this book has stimulated your interest in Yogācāra Buddhism even a little bit, this pleases me greatly, but at the same time, it is my sincere hope that you will carry your studies of this topic beyond the range of this book, on to a higher stage of expertise. For that purpose, I would like to recommend that you take a look at the suggestions for further reading provided by the translator.

Finally, I would like to extend my deep thanks to Mr. Moriya Okano of the Shunjusha editorial department who gave me valuable feedback while he tried to speed me up. I am slow about everything, and the reason I could finish this project in a somewhat timely fashion was due to these various supporting conditions.

Kohfukuji Temple, Bodai-in
March 24, 1989
Tagawa Shun'ei

Suggestions for Further Study

With the current state of availability of Yogācāra-related works in English, unfortunately, the new student to Yogācāra is forced to make a pretty big leap after reading an introductory book like this, as the rest of the relevant works that are presently available fall pretty much into the two categories of direct scriptural translation and detailed scholarly research. Nonetheless, with a bit of diligence and patience, one may certainly work to broaden one's grasp of Yogācāra by gradually working through what is presently available. Also, there is a fair amount of material freely available on the Internet that one may work through in small bites at one's own pace.

At the time of this writing, there are a number of dependable and informative scholarly works that provide thorough treatments of Yogācāra and related topics. A very comprehensive treatment is contained in Dan Lusthaus' *Buddhist Phenomenology*. This is a long and difficult text, but if you can slowly work through even some portions of it, you can go a long way toward advancing your grasp of Yogācāra Buddhism, especially in terms of the way it fits into the larger Buddhist tradition. Also published fairly recently is William Waldron's *The Buddhist Unconscious*. This book offers a detailed explanation of how the notion of *ālaya-vijñāna* arose from within the scheme of the Abhidharma six consciousnesses. You might also want to search for other interesting articles by Waldron for comparisons between Yogācāra and modern psychology, genetic theory, and so forth. Also helpful in its presentation of comparisons between Yogācāra and Western Psychology is Tao Jiang's *Contexts and Dialogue: Yogācāra Buddhism and Modern Psychology on the Subliminal Mind*.

For a thorough understanding of the historical course of development of the concept the *ālaya-vijñāna,* Lambert Schmithausen's 1977 book *Ālayavijñāna: On the Origin and the Early Development of a Central Concept of Yogācāra Philosophy* has become regarded as a classic work in the field. Many of Schmithausen's early hypotheses about the development of the *ālaya-vijñāna* have recently been challenged in an excellent book by Harmut Buescher entitled *The Inception of Yogācāra-Vijñānavāda.* Again, it takes some energy to work through these kinds of books, but if you can make it through even one of them, you'll come out with a solid grasp of the issues. For a reliable anthology of works that are attributed to Vasubandhu, see Thomas Kochumuttom's *A Buddhist Doctrine of Experience.*

Thanks to the efforts of the Bukkyō dendō kyōkai's [BDK] Numata Translation Series, some of the essential Yogācāra scriptural texts are coming into print. So far, John Keenan has translated the *Saṃdhinirmocana-sūtra* with the title *The Scripture on Explanation of the Underlying Meaning,* and the *Mahāyānasaṃgrāha* as *The Summary of the Great Vehicle.* Vasubandhu's influential *Triṃsikā* along with the *Cheng weishi lun* have been translated for the BDK by Frances Cook under the title of *Three Texts on Consciousness-only.* There are a number of other essential Yogācāra translations in progress in the BDK project, which are also now being released on the Web, so those interested in this field should keep abreast of their publications as they come out.

In the introduction of the above texts and authors, we have pretty much limited our scope to texts understood by the Faxiang and Tibetan schools to represent the orthodox Yogācāra view. But one's understanding of Yogācāra issues that deal with cognition, enlightenment, delusion, practice, and karma may also be enhanced through the study of works that have a close relation to Yogācāra, such as the *Laṅkāvatāra-sūtra,* or the *Awakening of Mahāyāna Faith,* or even some of the works produced within the Huayan school. On the Tibetan side, much of the discourse of the Tibetan tradition, and especially that of the Gelukpa school (the school of the present Dalai Lama), is strongly Yogācāra influenced, with great Tibetan masters such as Dzong-ka-ba dealing extensively in Yogācāra commentarial work. Also, the works of later Indian logicians such as Dharmakīrti dealt much with Yogācāra. If, after this point, you want to really get serious about studying Yogācāra, you'll need to begin learning some Asian languages! Best wishes in your continued studies of this rich topic.

A. Charles Muller
Tokyo, 2009

Notes

1. Tao Yuanming (365–427) was an eminent poet of the Eastern Jin, from the locale of Xunyang (in modern day Jiangxi). He is also found in reference works under the name Taoxian, with Yuanming being his pen-name. He referred to himself as Teacher Five Willows, and was called by others Teacher Jingjie. He was once a magistrate in the prefecture of Pengze, but quit after eighty days and returned home, expressing his feelings in a document called "Returning to Live in the Countryside." While farming, he delighted in wine and nature, playing the lute in the garden with his friends, and writing poetry. His works brought a major influence on subsequent literary forms. His extant works are collected in the *Tao Yuanming ji*.

2. The *Lucid Introduction* is a short text of just a couple pages, which lists all these mental factors. Written by Vasubandhu, it was translated into Chinese by Xuanzang as the *Dasheng baifa mingmen lun*, which is contained in the Japanese *Taishō Canon*, no. 1614.

3. A popular name for a chapter in the *Lotus Sūtra* entitled *Guanshiyin pusa pumen pin (Chapter of the Universal Gate of Avalokiteśvara Bodhisattva)*. The text states that Avalokiteśvara is capable of manifesting himself in thirty-three different bodies according to the states of the beings to be saved.

4. A sūtra understood to have been delivered by the Buddha as he was approaching his death, wherein he instructs his disciples, after his death, to uphold the precepts, guard the five senses, lessen the desires, seek equanimity, and cultivate concentration and wisdom.

5.   "Taint" here is a Buddhist technical term (Skt. *āsrava*) that indicates that some kind of intent is involved—that the fulfillment of some sort of desire, noble or ignoble, is anticipated.

6.   *Saikontan,* trans. by Usaburo Imai, Iwanami Classics Vol. 11 (Tokyo, 1973), p. 57.

7.   *Yuimagyō ni yoru bukkyō* ("Buddhism According to the *Vimalakīrti-sūtra*") (Osaka: Tōhō Shuppan, 1988).

8.   The *Cheng weishi lun (Discourse on the Theory of Consciousness-only)* was composed/edited/translated by the great Chinese Yogācāra master Xuanzang (600–664). It is widely regarded as the most comprehensive and systematic work on Yogācāra, presenting the views of a number of masters on all the basic Yogācāra topics. It is based primarily on Dharmapāla's commentary on the *Thirty Verses on Consciousness-only* (the *Triṃśikā-vijñapti-mātra śāstra*) by Vasubandhu. This text held great influence in East Asia, and especially in Japan, where the Japanese Hossō tradition bases its doctrine fully on this text. Thus, it is also the primary source for the presentation of the Yogācāra concepts made by Ven. Tagawa in this book. English versions include a rendering by Wei Tat of the French translation by Vallée Poussin. There is an English translation by Frances Cook in the Numata translation series, in the volume entitled *Three Texts on Consciousness-only*. This translation is not unuseful, but since Prof. Cook was not a Yogācāra specialist, it contains numerous errors and points of confusion, often at critical junctures. Thus, this vitally important text still awaits a thorough, careful translation by a Yogācāra specialist.

9.   Donation, observation of the precepts, forbearance, zeal, meditative concentration, and wisdom.

10.   Donation, kind words, altruistic activity, and working together with others.

11. Skt. *asmi-māna,* rendered by William Waldron as "the conceit 'I am,'" and by Lambert Schmithausen as simply "identity."

12. *The Two Fascicle Hossō Extracts,* "Grasping the Meaning."

13. From the *Memoranda of the Hall of Broad Learning (Tamon'in nikki),* ninth year of Tenshō (1581), twenty-ninth day of the twelfth lunar month. The *Tamon'in nikki* is a diary that was maintained over three dynastic periods at the Tamon'in, a subsidiary temple inside of Kōfukuji. Compilation was initiated by Eishun in 1478, and was maintained for 140 years, up to 1618.

14. From *The Way of the Housewife,* by Yamamoto Shūgorō *(Nihon fudō ki)* (Tokyo: Kodansha, 1968).
    (   )   (   )

15. This term comes directly from chapter 16 of the *Lotus Sutra,* "Chapter on the Longevity of the Tathāgata," wherein poisonous habituation refers to the karmic impressions of the three poisons. The author has published a modern Japanese study and translation of the Anthology of Rousing the Mind from Delusion, with the title *Jōkei: Gumei hosshin shū wo yomu: kokoro no yami wo mitsumeru (Jōkei's Anthology of Rousing the Mind from Delusion: Plumbing the Darkness of the Mind)* (Tokyo: Shunjūsha, 2004).

16. A tool similar to a sponge that is made from wrapping cotton with leather and cloth.

17. While it is true that Yogācāra does break down the two kinds of hindrances as being applicable to practitioners of the two vehicles and bodhisattvas, this distinction is only valid in a very general sense. Detailed examination of hindrance theory shows that this distinction is in fact much more tenuous. See A. Charles Muller, "The Yogācāra Two Hindrances and their Reinterpretations in East Asia," *Journal of the International Association of Buddhist*

Studies, Volume 27, Number 1 (2004), pp. 207–235. (Also available on the Web.)

18. In his book *Ryōgen and Mt. Hiei* (Hawaii UP, 2002), Paul Groner covers the content and events surrounding these debates in detail in chapter 6, "The Ōwa Debates."

19. From the *Kanjin i shōjō enmyō ji,* contained in the *Dai nihon bukkyō zensho,* vol. 80.

20. From the *Hossō Mind Essentials (Hossō shin yoshō), Taishō Canon,* no. 2311.

21. A reference to the *Bodhisattva-śīla sūtra,* contained in the *Taishō Canon,* no. 1501. Developed from excerpts from the *Yogācārabhūmi-śāstra* that explain the disciplines of the bodhisattva. This text served as the Yogācāra precepts manual, a routinely performed communal confession for monks and nuns.

22. The ten precepts are not killing, not stealing, not indulging in sexual excesses, not lying, not speaking divisively, not disparaging, not using ornate speech, not coveting, not giving way to anger, and not having false views.

23. The *Youxing jing* is a section of the *Dīrghāgama (Taishō Canon,* no. 1) In response to the questions by King Ajātaśatru regarding the handling of affairs with neighboring kingdoms, the Buddha explains the six and seven rules to the *bhikṣus*.

24. For example, see *Taishō Canon,* no. 1585.31.49a14–20.

About the Author

TAGAWA SHUN'EI, abbot of Kōfukuji, was born in 1947 in Nara. A graduate of Ritsumeikan University in Kyoto, he has spent his life as a Hossō monk in Kōfukuji, and is presently its abbot. In his extensive activity as a teacher and disseminator of Hossō doctrine, along with information regarding Kōfukuji (a world heritage cultural site) and its considerable store of cultural treasures, Ven. Tagawa stands out among modern-day Japanese Buddhist monks. As one can tell from reading this book, his mastery of Yogācāra doctrine is deep, and he is especially well-studied in the works of the earlier monks of the Hossō lineage, having published, for example, in 2004, the book *Jōkei: Gumei hosshin shū wo yomu* ("Jōkei: A Reading of the Anthology of the Mind Arisen from Foolishness"; Tokyo, Shunjūsha). He has been running for several years a regular lecture series that alternates, on approximately a biweekly basis, between Nara and Tokyo, consisting of lectures on Buddhist art and culture by academic specialists, along with lectures on Yogācāra delivered by himself and noted Japanese researchers of *yuishiki*.

A. CHARLES MULLER, translator, is a professor in the Graduate School of Humanities and Sociology at the University of Tokyo. He is the translator for *The Sūtra of Perfect Enlightenment: Korean Buddhism's Guide to Meditation* (SUNY Press, 1999), and is founder and managing editor of both the *Digital Dictionary of Buddhism* and the H-Buddhism Buddhist Scholars Information Network.

About Wisdom Publications

WISDOM PUBLICATIONS, a nonprofit publisher, is dedicated to making available authentic works relating to Buddhism for the benefit of all. We publish books by ancient and modern masters in all traditions of Buddhism, translations of important texts, and original scholarship. Additionally, we offer books that explore East-West themes unfolding as traditional Buddhism encounters our modern culture in all its aspects. Our titles are published with the appreciation of Buddhism as a living philosophy, and with the special commitment to preserve and transmit important works from Buddhism's many traditions.

To learn more about Wisdom, or to browse books online, visit our website at www.wisdompubs.org.

You may request a copy of our catalog online or by writing to this address:

Wisdom Publications
199 Elm Street
Somerville, Massachusetts 02144 USA
Telephone: 617-776-7416
Fax: 617-776-7841
Email: info@wisdompubs.org
www.wisdompubs.org

THE WISDOM TRUST

As a nonprofit publisher, Wisdom is dedicated to the publication of Dharma books for the benefit of all sentient beings and dependent upon the kindness and generosity of sponsors in order to do so. If you would like to make a donation to Wisdom, you may do so through our website or our Somerville office. If you would like to help sponsor the publication of a book, please write or email us at the address above.

Thank you.

Wisdom is a nonprofit, charitable 501(c)(3) organization affiliated with the Foundation for the Preservation of the Mahayana Tradition (FPMT).